Fit-For-Purpose
Leadership #1

LeadershipGigs

WRITING MATTERS PUBLISHING

Fit-For-Purpose Leadership #1

First published in 2017

Writing Matters Publishing (UK)
info@writingmatterspublishing.com
www.writingmatterspublishing.com

ISBN 978-0-9956051-9-0

Editor: Andrew Priestley

Contributors: Karen Ingram, Peter Allton, Neil D'Silva, Dom Mason, Elizabeth Banks, Sarah-Anne Lucas, Sean Foley, Joy Zarine, Daniel Browne, Tara Halliday, Robert James, Ben Green, Padma Coram, David Sammel, Hilary McGowan, Susan Payton, Antoinette Oglethorpe, Andrew Priestley

Dedication

Dedicated to leaders everywhere - and to you -
someone who has decided to step-up and positively change
the world, or *your* world. It is especially dedicated
to the new breed of leader that is lean, clean and clear.

Contents

About Leadership Gigs

Leadership Gigs was launched in January 2017 as a global, invitation-only, *WhatsApp* community, for business leaders - CEOs, MDs, executives, business owners and entrepreneurs.

This unique community was created in response to the need of leaders in senior positions for open, authentic conversations with peers. Most leaders don't feel it's appropriate to have that level of self-disclosing openness with work colleagues, who look up to them as confident, infallible leaders.

The forum works because it allows them to have totally confidential discussions about problems and challenges with their peers from a broad and diverse range of industries.

The glue is *Trust*.

Leadership Gigs offers a safe forum for bouncing ideas off one another, sharing, discussing, reflecting and receiving candid, constructive feedback. But importantly it allows them to de-role, share concerns, doubts, express vulnerability and get support. Feedback suggests that being able to talk freely with other business leaders reduces stress and isolation and leads to insights, breakthroughs and key light bulb moments.

The calibre of leaders and the open, candid exchange in *Leadership Gig*s is truthful, practical, insightful and above all, truly inspiring.

The New Breed of Leaders: Lean, Clean and Clear

Andrew Priestley

For the past five years we've observed the emerging global *corporate wellness and wellbeing* trend in America and in the UK. A growing number of businesses are adapting their workplace cultures to incorporate principles of health and ergonomics; but increasingly wellness and emotional wellbeing for their staff.

According to the *Chartered Institute of Personnel and Development* (CIPD) it was estimated that UK businesses lost an average of 6.9 days per employee to *absenteeism*. And 23% of UK businesses reported a rise in *non-genuine absenteeism* (*pulling a sickie*). Conservatively, CIPD estimates the cost to the UK economy in excess of £100bn. The survey (2016) also noted associated decreases in *productivity*.

As a general principle the average UK professional works 37.5 hours per week x 45 weeks a year - essentially, 1687.5 hours per annum. Of course no-one is 100% productive.

As a rule of thumb if productivity drops below 42% - 708.75 productive hours – that business is in trouble. And if an employee is pushed beyond 80% we observe increased stress and burnout.

The optimum level of *productivity* is around 72% or 1215

productive hours. No wonder there is concern when the *average* productivity rate is 43%. And at the leadership level, absenteeism and a drop in productivity, becomes even more significant.

There is growing concern as *NHS* spending has increased annually on average from 8.8 % to 10.1% of GDP since 2000.

According to the UK *Labour Force Survey* (2016) work-related stress, depression and anxiety caused absenteeism totalling 11.7 million days; an average of 24 stress leave days per worker in one year. This figure sounds unbelievably high but it is a conservative estimate.

In 2015, stress accounted for 45% of all working days lost due to ill health. Stress is more prevalent in public service industries, such as education, health and social care and public administration and defence.

The main factors causing work-related stress, depression or anxiety were workload pressures, tight deadlines, too much responsibility and a lack of managerial or employer support.

In companies where corporate wellness initiatives are implemented we see a reversal of these trends. It therefore makes commercial sense to encourage employees to be healthy and emotionally resilient.

Initially, corporate wellness and wellbeing extended to *ergonomics* (furniture, lighting, noise) and culturally healthy workplace environments (diversity, sexism, bullying); then employee health initiatives (flexible hours, health screenings and gym memberships).

While these initiatives were made available they show up as *policy*; or *take-it-or-leave-it* passive offerings.

But the emerging trend appears to be an increase in employees *wanting* to live a healthier lifestyle, rather than being coaxed, cajoled or coerced to do so.

And employees opting for workplace environments and cultures where health and wellbeing are not token gestures.

Simple research on *preferred employers of choice* is revealing.

Five years ago the focus was on career path, pay, conditions and employee benefits but a recent review by the *Top Employers Institute* (2017) shows social responsibility, L&D opportunities, diversity, healthcare, culture, values, *Millennial*-friendly work-life balance, collaboration and community are prominent qualities professionals are now seeking.

We know that wellness and wellbeing cultures work best when the experience is appreciated and shared. And even more effectively when management and executives *authentically* choose to actively model these values to employees.

In the top 5% of executive talent we are observing a new breed of ambitious leader who is *lean, clean* and *clear* - actively pursuing meaningful outcomes.

Lean means trimmed down, in shape where there is an obvious commitment to good health. Basically, leaders that *look the business*.

The top 5% talent is looking slim, fit and full of vitality. And subsequently, businesses are trimming down as well. Not only are companies hiring smarter, they are hiring *fitter* players who are *fit-for-purpose* in more ways that one.

Leanne Spencer (*Rise and Shine,* 2016) of *Bodyshot Performance* in the UK has noted a steady increase in busy, time-poor, professionals seeking a fast track to good health.

She specialises in DNA screening that gives her clients laser focus clarity about the best diets and exercise regimes. More city workers are wanting peak health. Instead of going for a beer, savvy, ambitious professionals are increasingly opting to go for a run or a workout with colleagues.

Increasingly, employees *want* to work in a *clean* culture.

Clean means just that. The new breed leader is increasingly drug and alcohol free. Obviously, *liquid lunches* are long gone but there is a growing trend to not tolerate employees with alcohol and recreational drug issues - especially executives.

Sam Carpenter (*Work The System*, 2012) runs a private emergency call centre in the USA. His staff *have to* be clean. Employees undergo random toxicology tests several times a year. Sam simply cannot afford to have someone hung-over or stoned take an inbound medical emergency call where poor response time equates to lives lost!

Clear means *on-message, on-game* and *on-purpose.*

Top 5% executives want more meaningful work and are leaning towards greater clarity of the vision and values of their employers and are opting for *gigs* where there's an obvious alignment.

We are also seeing a rise in corporate citizenship.

In line with the Bill Gates challenge to *Do Well, Do Good* manifesto companies like *Buy1Give1* (Singapore) and *Dent* (UK) have embraced as a highly visible, unifying all-in, team philosophy that embraces initiatives like the *United Nations Global Goals.*

More companies are donating a significant percentage of revenues to solve *meaningful problems*. For example, projects that deliver clean water and sanitation, end hunger and protect the environment.

The remit is clear: the company must exist for more than revenues and profits. More companies now exist to deliver sustainable results and solve major problems in the wider world.

Award-winning executive interim recruiter, Pat Lynes (*The Interim Revolution*, 2017) from *Sullivan & Stanley*, London has identified a dominant trend in top flight executives consciously seeking meaning in the job and fulfillment of the ultimate objective of life through work.

His observation is top 5% talent are turning down *gigs* that do not tick that *meaningful work* box. The *executive gig economy* seems to be about being *on-purpose*.

A huge disruptive workplace trend is *Millennial attrition*.

A CIPD 2017 survey showed that 60% of *Millennials* do not leave a good company – they leave a *bad boss* - especially bosses who treat them as *units of labour* rather than partners in a broader journey for fulfillment.

As a result, fit-for-purpose *Millennials* are voting with their feet and *sprinting* away from sluggish, dowdy companies and bad bosses.

Fit-For Purpose Leadership explores these growing trends.

We identified six key themes for leadership/workplace innovation: *health, mindset, social/culture, meaning and purpose, best-practice/peak performance* and *emerging trends*.

In 2017, we created a global, invitation-only leadership forum called *Leadership Gigs* that has attracted what we feel is the new-breed of leader who is authentically pursuing peak performance in these key areas.

With that in mind we issued a challenge: *let's write a book*.

Our members were asked to share their highest value advice in one powerful article that would genuinely benefit the emerging new-breed, fit-for-purpose leader. You will not be disappointed.

In these pages you possess gold nuggets from a solid line-up of successful leaders at the top of their game sharing their best thinking and potent strategies to create profound results.

- In *Health*, Karen Ingram (#GoOffGrid), Peter Allton *(Type II Diabetes),* Dom Mason (executive energy), Sarah-Anne Lucas (effective health rituals for busy professionals), Neil D'Silva (nutrition and gut health) and Elizabeth Banks (get moving).

- In *Mindset*, Sean Foley (emotional intelligence), Joy Zarine (*five star* thinking) and Daniel Browne (focus).

- In *Social*, Robert James (work/life balance) and Tara Halliday (on *Impostor Syndrome).*

- In *Meaning and Purpose*, Ben Green (the *Dao* of leadership) and Padma Coram (*Chakra* meditation).

- In *Best Practice*, David Sammel (building leadership teams) and Hilary McGowan (astute leadership).

- In *Trends*, Susan Payton (why your story matters), Antoinette Oglethorpe (leadership vs management) and Andrew Priestley (what highly effective leaders do under pressure).

Fit-For-Purpose Leadership #1 makes compelling reading.

Think: *five star*. Think: *smartcuts*. Think: *A-Game* and *A-Team*. Think: value-based leadership, agile, stewardship and servant leader. Think: *lean, clean* and *clear* and you have the essence of the new breed fit-for-purpose leader.

Health

Physical health, fitness, exercise, wellness, wellbeing, nutrition, diet, exercise, nutrition, sleep, hydration, hormones, genetics, DNA

Get Moving and Go Off Grid

Karen Ingram

When I was four, my dad gave up his paid job and set up his own business as an insurance broker.

For the first few years his office was in our dining room, so work was everywhere, which drove my mum mad. From a young age I was trained to answer the home phone, "Hello, GML insurance brokers!"

This was well before the days of email and internet, but at home I remember a constant work presence. Even when we were on holiday my Dad would sneak off to a call box to make *essential* phone calls. After he opened offices and had staff, he used to ring the office at least once a day when we were on holiday. For a short time after these phone calls you could tell he was distracted and not really *with* us.

Having run my own business for 16 years and with all the blessings and curses of modern technology, I can now imagine how my Dad would have felt.

It is so easy to think, 'I will just check my emails, it will only take five minutes'.

What you forget is that for the next two hours you are stewing over the one email you read from an unhappy customer or worrying about the post on *Facebook* from a competitor, announcing they are opening up just down the road from you.

These days it is all too easy to be tuned into work 24/7.

As business leaders, we focus on the things we do, our productivity, knowledge, awareness of our sector, building networks, constantly communicating. Instead I would like you to take some time to think about how often, or not, you 'don't do'!

There is increasing evidence to suggest that being *always on* - constantly online and available - is detrimental to your health. It can lead to being stressed out, exhausted and perpetually teetering on the brink of a cold, or something worse, because your immune system is being fried.

Stress, in the right amount, is a good thing, it can help you perform under pressure. It can bring energy, keep you fired up, and help you focus.

Tip into too much stress, or never take a break from stress and you can feel frazzled and overwhelmed. If you constantly operate in emergency mode then your body and mind will suffer. Beyond a certain point, stress stops being helpful and starts damaging your health. Too much stress will affect your mood, your productivity, your relationships, and ultimately your quality of life.

When triggered, the body's *stress response* floods you with stress hormones. Two of the main hormones are *adrenaline* and *cortisol*. Together these hormones get you ready to run or fight, making your heart pound, tightening muscles, increasing blood pressure and quickening your breath.

Adrenaline gives you a surge of energy; and cortisol redirects your bodies resources, for example, slowing down digestion and suppressing your immune system.

Unfortunately, our bodies don't know the difference between a true life and death situation, like coming face to face with a tiger that's escaped from the zoo, or a pressing work deadline. The physiological response is the same.

The underlying danger of stress is that *you get used to it.*

After a while we all stop noticing that we are constantly a little bit *wired.* Plus, the more your stress system is activated the harder it becomes to shut it off.

For me having a happy and a profitable business are not mutually exclusive. My sustainable good mental and physical health are critical elements of my ability to lead successfully and to enjoying the process.

I want to share two strategies for thriving as a leader in this modern *always on* world. The first helps you immediately deal with stress and the second makes you carve out and value down time in order to reduce stress:

- Get Moving
- Go Off Grid

Get Moving!

Physically moving, in whatever way you enjoy has an immediate and positive effect on stress.

Our fight or flight mode is an ancient system in response to a physical threat, it generates masses of energy. You see a tiger and run like mad! In modern-day life threat or stress is usually more psychological and so we don't get the opportunity to burn this energy off.

Regular exercise helps to reduce cortisol levels in the body and you can burn off adrenaline with cardiovascular exercise. Exercise also pumps up your endorphin levels, the *feel-good* neurotransmitters in our bodies.

Whilst cardiovascular exercise is best for reducing adrenaline, you will still reduce stress levels with something as simple as a rhythmic walk, as low intensity as Pilates or yoga as well as a full-on *High Intensity Training* (HIT session).

Exercise like Pilates requires the mind and body to connect and for you to focus on the movements you are making. This can act a bit like meditation, stilling the mind. Walking can have a similar effect. I regularly practice Pilates and also run. But if I'm really feeling the pressure I go to this class in our local gym where they play loud rock music and I get to hit tractor tyres with a sledgehammer!

Exercise can also improve your sleep, which is often disrupted by stress. If you begin to regularly shake off your daily stresses through movement and physical activity, you may find that this focus on a single physical task, and the resulting energy and positivity, can help you remain calm in your leadership role.

Go Off Grid

For me the bigger challenge is the second of my two strategies for thriving as a leader in this modern *always on* world: *going off grid*. I have two *off grid* rules:

- You must take holidays and your holiday must be 100% free of business.
- Take at least one day off a week that is 100% free of business.

So here is the challenge, can you genuinely *go off grid*:

Only me and my family

Free 100% of business

Free from all social media: *Facebook, Twitter, LinkedIn, What'sApp, Messenger!*

Get new perspective

Refresh mind, body and spirit

Inspire, get new ideas

Dare to be unavailable

When you are a leader in business it is all too easy to give and give, always prioritising the business over your needs.

It is essential you build in proper time where you can re-charge. Carve out at least one or two full weeks in a block to have a holiday. Spend time with just friends or family and do nothing what so ever that relates to business.

I want to share two examples of how not to do this. I work with a husband and wife team who have their own dental practice, their annual winter holiday is a ski trip to the French Alps. The ski trip is part of a dental convention and they ski with other dentists, talk shop all week and attend lectures!

On the business park where our studio is based is an amazing camping shop, run by a passionate husband and wife team. Their annual holiday is camping in the Cotswolds, at an *Outdoor Trade Show*, where they do all their buying for the upcoming year!

Remember, it is not a holiday unless you go off grid and it is genuinely 100% business free.

The same is true for your one business free day a week.

This does not mean two half days or taking a morning off, because you are working that evening. This means 24 hours of total and absolute *nothing to do with work*.

For me this is nearly always a Sunday, and if for some reason I am working on a Sunday, I keep the Monday free instead.

At the end of the working day and definitely during your time off, you should turn your mobile phone into a *dumb* phone and ignore all the other communication devices on it.

Days off and holidays should be technology free, so no emails, *Facebook*, internet, etc. I turn the emails off on my phone, delete the *Facebook* and other social media *Apps* and don't go anywhere near the internet. At first it feels really tough, but after a while your body and your mind will thank you for it.

When your business is *closed* and it is outside office hours, *unplug from technology* and engage with your physical surroundings.

It will help you to rest your brain and to feel refreshed when the next working day starts.

I love *active holidays*. It's pretty hard to check your emails when you running or skiing or windsurfing!

I love being outdoors and it always puts things into perspective. Walking up a mountain reminds me that there is more to life than running a Pilates business and that we are just small little dots on a very big planet!

I get some of my best ideas when I'm away from work and away from technology. If a business idea pops into my head while I'm on holiday then I use the voice recorder on my phone, quickly capture my idea, and then forget all about it and get on with my time off.

The secret is to let business thoughts that drift into your brain just drift off again. Try not to start over-thinking or worrying about issues.

Do your best to let it go!

If you are going to stay good at what you do, focused and enthusiastic, you have to have *complete breaks*.

Some of the most successful business leaders in the world also relish their leisure time. Look at Richard Branson for example.

You will find that genuine time away from your leadership role will give you a new perspective. Your mind and body will have the opportunity to be refreshed and your stress system will be rested. Genuine down time can inspire you with new ideas and in turn help you to inspire the people you lead when you are back in leadership mode.

So dare to be unavailable.

Put an out of office message on your email.

Put a sign up on social media saying your unavailable for a couple of weeks, change your *answerphone* message to say you are shut.

If you are genuinely worried that you might miss out on the deal of a lifetime while you are on holiday then ask someone to monitor your messages for you. If you are a sole trader with no other staff then there are some great virtual PA services out there. You could also ask someone you trust to deal with enquiries while you are away.

It is completely healthy and permissible to turn your back on your business for periods of time and to enjoy your family, friends and the things you love to do. It will reignite your passion for why you are a leader in business.

So grab your diary and schedule time in your week to *get moving* and block out a weeks holiday and *#Go Off Grid*.

Karen Ingram is an accomplished business leader and mentor in the fitness sector. She is a co-founder of *Barefoot Studio*, a leading UK Pilates studio, activewear store and wellness centre, an instructor, trainer and international presenter on both Pilates and business.

She is a best selling author, and her book *Thrive Don't Just Survive* combines her passion for inspiring others and for business.

Karen runs a teacher training academy that takes people new to teaching and gives them the skills to become successful Pilates instructors and business owners. Working in the health and fitness sector, Karen is passionate about business leaders working in a way that is not just profitable but enjoyable, balanced and life enhancing.

Phone	*+ 44 (0)1446 775 772*
Web	*www.kareningramacademy.co.uk*
	www.barefootstudio.co.uk
Email	*info@kareningramacademy.co.uk*

Walk Your Talk

Peter Allton

As leaders we are called to walk our talk being trustworthy and full of integrity wanting the absolute best for those we have the privilege of leading. What benefit would it be to your mentee to become the world's best in their field of business only to find they have a preventable lifestyle disease that could rob them of precious years of good health?

For the first time ever in the history of humanity the most common cause of death globally has become lifestyle diseases and diabetes itself accounts for one every six seconds.

Additionally every 20 seconds someone with diabetes has a lower limb amputation which then means they have an 80% likelihood of not surviving the subsequent five years. This is a shockingly unnecessary waste of life and ability as 85% could be avoided and the deaths postponed.

95% of diabetes cases are *Type II* caused by lifestyle choices and the majority of those are preceded by years of the person often unknowingly being *Pre-diabetic*.

Let me challenge you to read this chapter in its entirety however unlikely you think you are to develop *diabetes*.

Statistically in the UK one out of three of your circle of friends and associates will either have *pre-diabetes*, *undiagnosed diabetes* or *diabetes*.

We should with humility all ask ourselves the following three questions:

- How sure am I that I'm not pre-diabetic or diabetic?
- And how sure am I that I won't be at my next milestone birthday?
- Should leading my people include caring for them enough to at least point them towards an awareness of their health?

I believe all leaders should take an interest in their client's and team's welfare. Does this mean that the marketing genius or the sales expert have to directly teach their mentee not only in their specialty but also in healthcare – of course not but it should mean they're living a healthy disciplined life and encouraging their clients to do the same.

Medics will often refer to the importance of a multidisciplinary team to get maximum benefit for their patient and so too we should have a team of colleagues willing to step in and do their bit for each other's clients.

Let me tell you the story of John

John A is a typical 41 year old British man living in suburban London, a father of four children and with a devoted wife.

Our story begins earlier in life. John at an early age had become accustomed to the taste of sweetness and later as a student the lure of pizza and other fast foods became not the norm but certainly a regular source of *nutrition*.

In early life he was quite active playing sports and running regularly and so this diet didn't seem to be having much effect. Behind the scenes however the likelihood was that this carbohydrate rich diet was in fact not only gradually increasing his waistline but also slowly adding internal fat to his organs such as the liver and pancreas.

As the years went by John A married and had a family, life became increasingly busy and gradually without him really being aware his amount of activity decreased whilst his calorie intake increased fuelled largely by comfort eating during times of stress and the bad habit of snacking especially whilst driving the one hour to and from work.

The combined result was significant weight gain.

From time to time John would make an effort to drag himself out of the pit he felt he had fallen into by buying a new pair of running shoes and making a token effort to get fit. However he would almost always not make it into the second month.

He became an expert at making excuses, too busy, too tired, its late, too cold, too hot etc.

This lack of exercise was certainly having an effect on his health but unbeknown to him the biggest factor was his diet. Seemingly healthy he had cut out added sugar and always opted for diet drinks. He loved his vegetables, ate meat in moderation and welcomed a good portion of spuds, rice or pasta. In fact he loved his food so much he would usually have seconds.

This continued on for a number of years and his weight gradually increased until he finally tipped the scales at 100 kg. This milestone in life coincided with his 40th birthday and it wasn't long after that he was diagnosed with *Type II diabetes*.

Then followed seven years of trying to manage his blood sugars firstly by trying to watch what and how much he ate, which seemed to work initially.

However eventually he had to give in to the GP's advice that medication was needed.

This seemed to maintain the blood sugars but as time went by the dosage had to go up and it became apparent that his diabetes was not controlled and was in fact likely to be beginning to affect his eyes, his feet and kidneys not to mention the cardiovascular system as a whole. In fact it became obvious that he needed not only medication for diabetes but also for blood pressure and high cholesterol.

John B was always a smartly turned out chap who could usually be seen sporting a suit and a pair of immaculate shiny brogues.

So here we have him shortly after his 47th birthday seated in the hospital waiting room of the podiatry clinic in his usual attire except that on his left foot was a rather oversized slipper with its toe end of the upper cut out –a stark comparison to the shiny brogue on his right.

He had been having to attend the clinic every Monday, Wednesday and Friday for the past five months, ever since a small pressure area from a rather pointed new pair of shoes had caused a small wound that had then become infected. He had learned that his diabetes had damaged his blood supply and nerves, causing a loss of sensation and that was why he hadn't even noticed the problem with the shoes. He was experiencing the inconvenience of having it dressed every few days and had been told there was no hope of the toe ever recovering. Indeed that day as his big toe was unveiled from its dressing to reveal its dark dry mummified appearance, half of it came away in the podiatrist's hands.

John is my middle name and John A is me.

John B was my patient and his toe dropping off was the first time I ever encountered gangrene. It wasn't so much the sight of half the toe falling off that hit me as much as the realisation that he was in his prime of life – I was shocked and found myself wondering how this would affect his quality of life, his ability to go on long walks with his wife, enjoy a round of golf, to play with his son or even to walk his daughter down the aisle.

My personal journey and of people like John B have made me realise how easily bad habits formed over decades can rob you of a good quality of life being able to do the things you enjoy with your loved ones.

One in three of us is either at risk of or has *Type II Diabetes* and so absolutely you will know people who have it. The chances are they may not have told you and of course they may be one of the 50% of people with diabetes who are unaware they have it.

Unfortunately this usually means that by the time you are diagnosed there is substantial damage to the nerve endings and blood vessels meaning they are often well on their way to diabetic complications such as effects on the eyes, kidneys, heart and the extremities (especially the feet).

As leaders we should live healthily ditching bad habits and encouraging those we lead to do the same, (spouses, family, friends, colleagues, employees or clients).

The best way to help them is to get them to live in what I call the *Diabetic Sweet Spot (DSS)* - a place where they are at best free of diabetes and at worst have the condition but are managing their high blood sugars well.

See *www.undefeeted.org/book.html*

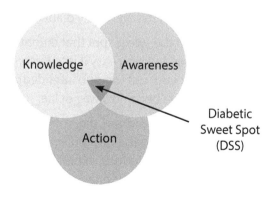

In a nutshell to be safe in the *DSS* you need to have three things.

- As much knowledge as possible of the disease and its effects
- An awareness of the risk you are at of having it, developing it , or having complications because of it.
- A willingness to take whatever action is necessary to prevent it, reverse it or prevent complications from it.

Just as in golf you have to hit the sweet spot of the club to make the best shot so too in life you need to live in the sweet spot to have the best chances of:

- Preventing diabetes
- Reversing diabetes
- Living with your diabetes but with your blood sugars really well controlled

Thankfully my story did not end up like John B but could very easily have done so .

I knew all there was to know about diabetes and its devastating effects and I had a good idea of my personal risk of complications. And yet despite seeing firsthand the gruesome effects of the disease the final cog in the machine was missing- taking action to reverse my diabetes.

It was my journey into the sweet spot that taught me so much about human behaviour and how easy it is to become ensnared into different vices that your gut (no pun intended) tells you are wrong but that over years become a way of life.

You may be reading this, and as I did, make the decision to go all-in once and for all to get a grip on your health. Perhaps you are carrying a few more pounds, experiencing some of the symptoms of diabetes such as tiredness, thirst or going to the loo more often and have like so many people just thought of it as normal aging or the effects of stress.

Although there is one easy formula to get you or your mentee into the *DSS* it is very much an individual journey and in my experience requires personalised guidance (to set *SMART* goals) and the all important accountability (to ensure the correct action is taken.)

Too many of us live many years perfecting various terrible habits, living a sedentary lifestyle and eating too many calories in a carbohydrate rich diet and it is this that causes lifestyle diseases such as diabetes.

Great self discipline is required to change and that fact alone is in my mind the reason why I believe whatever leadership role you are in demands you to set an example in the discipline of leading a healthy life yourself.

So let me challenge, encourage, and commend you as appropriate to make sure you commit to leading that healthy life. Be real with yourself and encourage your mentees to be so too. It can be hard when you're in your 20s or 30s to have a clear vision of what you may look like in the future but I would encourage you to try to picture yourself with another 10-20 years behind you and ask yourself *"What will I look like if I carry on living the way I am now?".*

You may be someone who is motivated by fear of what might happen in which case that approach might work or conversely you may be someone who is motivated by the positives of what you want to be able to achieve in which case take a moment to write down a timeline of your remaining life and plot at different stages what you want to achieve and still be able to do in each decade of life.

Identify the changes you need to make and then crucially put in place the resources you need to ensure you follow through and make them.

True character will be shown and indeed formed by committing to these actions and doing whatever it takes to ensure you stay on the path of change. This is where you need to admit to yourself the need for help and guidance and expect the same of your mentee.

Personally living with diabetes for seven years and experiencing two failed attempts to reverse it gave me great insights into the challenges involved in changing the habits built up over 40 years.

It was only by applying the principles of the *Diabetic Sweet Spot* reinforced by having people in my life holding me accountable that I have been able to reverse my diabetes and maintain non diabetic blood sugars without any medication for the past year. That means I can now stand firmly in the *Diabetic Sweet Spot* confident that my blood sugar levels are not gradually killing me and robbing me of precious years with my family or affecting my ability to live my later years fully able to do all I want to in life. Indeed my diabetes reversal diet has ensured I don't need any of my medications for diabetes, blood pressure or high cholesterol any longer.

Let me leave you to ponder this question: If you had a diagnosis of cancer tomorrow how seriously would you take your health? In my experience most of us would do all it takes to try to overcome it.

You would be unlikely to say *"I have a touch of cancer"* yet that's the attitude often with people when diagnosed with diabetes. Would you be content saying I have pre-cancer? Probably not so why do so many people have pre-diabetes and not do anything about it.

I am committed through my global not for profit organisation *www.undefeeted.org* to preventing diabetes related lower limb amputations that currently happen every 20 seconds.

To make our vision of cutting that rate to one a minute by 2035 it is essential that people around the world are taught how diabetes can affect them, understand their risk and then act to minimise that risk. The number 1 way to ensure minimum risk is to have optimum control of blood sugars and for pre-diabetes or *Type II Diabetes* that means reversing it.

I mentor people to do just that through *Undefeeted's ideal diabetic lifestyle* and its my team's mission to mentor you and your families, friends and clients to live lives that are safe from the dangers of high blood sugars thus ensuring you don't develop pre-diabetes or *Type II Diabetes* with its associated debilitating and often fatal effects.

Thus you will be able to live life to the full continuing to do the things you enjoy with those you love for many years to come.

Peter Allton is a qualified Podiatrist with over 30 years experience his career took a change of emphasis when in 2009 he was diagnosed with *Type-II Diabetes*. Two years later his then 11 year old daughter developed *Type-I*.

Thus Peter's passion was ignited to make a difference in the lives of people with diabetes. In 2015, he published his book *Undefeeted By Diabetes* and co-founded the multi-award winning global not-for-profit organisation *Undefeeted*.

Attracting worldwide attention *Undefeeted* has received interest from many countries where they aim to help put into place systems to help reduce the prevalence of diabetes and the complications that so often lead to amputations.

The *Undefeeted* vision is to see the current rate of one amputation every 20 seconds be slashed by two thirds to one a minute by 14th November, 2035.

Peter Allton

Undefeeted HQ

3 Hoskins Road Oxted Surrey UK RH8 9HT

Contact@undefeeted.org

+44 (0) 207 112 9210

Optimal Nutrition, Energy and Health

Neil D'Silva

Energy - that invisible force of nature that we have in abundance when we are young, but as we age our energy levels can decline until we can get to the point of exhaustion or burn-out.

This is a problem for most people, and can become a serious issue for those that run their own business or for those in demanding senior positions. A lack of energy affects performance, which can have consequences for your company and for those around you.

Good health can be measured in two ways:

- the absence of disease and related symptoms; and
- how you feel and perform, both mentally and physically.

There are many factors related to how we feel both physically and mentally, and what you consume is amongst the most influential to these.

Energy levels can be improved if you know what action to take.

Your body is built from the food you consume – these include the major influencers of your health; carbohydrates, fats, proteins, water, vitamins and minerals. Every cell and organ of your body is affected by your diet, as the energy provided supplies the building blocks needed to construct and maintain them.

The food you eat is metabolised by the cells of your body – be that food nutrient-dense or nutrient-deficient.

The importance of obtaining energy from nutrient-rich and not from nutrient-deficient sources is borne out by a simple illustration.

Imagine two builders, each looking to build a house for themselves.

Builder one understands that the longevity and quality of the house depends on having proper foundations, using good quality building materials and adherence to a well thought-out, logical blueprint. He wants a house to be proud of, one that will last and that will not be a chore to maintain.

Builder two, on the other hand, is not bothered about digging proper foundations, after all, that is just too much effort. And as for the materials, well anything cheap will do. The house might look OK once it is built, so no-one will know the difference. Just get it built quickly, why worry about what might happen in five or ten years time?

What house would you rather live in? One with decent foundations, is built with care and attention with good quality materials by a conscientious, knowledgeable builder. Or the house that looks OK, but the workmanship was shoddy at best, built on a budget and with inferior materials?

Well, you are the builder and the house is your body.

Fuel it properly and on a regular basis with good quality, high nutrient foods, and it will perform better for longer. It will be easier to maintain good health and you will enjoy improved energy levels and other benefits.

Consistently eat low nutrient, high calorie, high sugar junk food and you are the house built with cheap, inferior materials. Indeed, the house might be OK for a while, but the effort required to keep it standing is going to be more than a house built properly. Eventually, time will catch up with the inferior house, and it is likely to be the one that falls first.

The future catches up with us all at some point.

Our habits and lifestyle here and now will have a massive influence on our future-self and future-health – for better or for worse. It is an interesting exercise to think ahead as to how your current diet, lifestyle and habits might impact your own health in the years to come. A lot of illnesses (including Type II Diabetes, Cancers and Cardiovascular Disease) develop over time. A person doesn't wake up one morning with these diseases, they can take many years to manifest.

If your current diet and lifestyle supports a happy, energetic and healthy life then I encourage you to keep up the good work. If, after reading this piece, you feel that improvements need to be made to enjoy a healthier life now and in the future, then decide today to make those changes.

Remember, when it comes to improving your health, every step in the right direction is a step in the right direction, no matter how small.

Six simple ways to improve your health and energy levels

There are many ways in which you can improve your health and energy levels, and I have chosen six key areas for you to review and to improve on.

These are not recommendations, nor should be followed without first consulting your healthcare professional. I do believe, however, that if even one or more of these are followed consistently and regularly, then an improvement in energy levels and your overall health should result.

1. Cut out refined sugar in all its forms

Sugar is *empty calories*, containing no essential nutrients – no proteins, no fats, no vitamins and no minerals.

Sugar comes in the white granular form that we know, but it is also added to over 80% of foods on supermarket shelves in one form or another (including Agave Nectar, Galactose, Glucose, Maltodextrin, Corn Syrup, Fructose, Glucose, High Fructose Corn Syrup (HFCS), Honey, Invert Sugar, Maltose, Lactose, Dextrose, Sucrose … the list goes on).

Simply looking for *sugar* on a food label is no longer a safeguard against its consumption – you need to identify the *hidden sugars* in the food you eat.

Many people lead relatively sedentary lives and therefore have no need for the additional rush of energy that sugar provides. This excess energy can lead to weight gain and obesity, as well as contributing to some unpleasant conditions including Insulin resistance (a precursor for Type II Diabetes), Cancers and Cardiovascular Disease.

Sugar is also incredibly addictive and, amongst other issues, it blocks Leptin (the hormone that tells you when you are full) which can then lead to over-eating.

Reduce your sugar consumption by making informed choices about the foods you eat and the fluids you drink, and never add sugar to your food or drink. I am not an advocate of artificial sweeteners as a long-term sugar substitute, and advise my clients to cut back on sugar completely over time.

The biggest objection to cutting out sugar is for taste reasons, and I suggest that gradual and consistent changes are made. For example: reduce the number of sugars in your hot drinks by half a teaspoon per month. Your taste buds will adjust accordingly, and it is perfectly possible for someone taking three teaspoons of sugar in their tea to cut down to zero over six months.

2. Drink more water

Your body comprises of around 60% water. Water has no calories and does not provide energy for the body. What water does do is to hydrate you and helps your cells to function properly. It fuels your metabolism, regulates your body temperature, lubricates your joints, transports nutrients around your body, helps to curb hunger pangs, helps to energise muscles, keeps your skin looking good, helps your kidneys to function properly, helps maintain normal bowel function… I could continue but suffice to say that adequate water is essential to maintaining good health.

Dehydration can have a serious negative affect on the body: impaired energy levels and thinking ability, increased levels of Cortisol (potentially causing elevated stress levels and depression), increased blood pressure and heart rate, digestive problems, heartburn, joint pain, kidney issues, decreased muscle mass and continual hunger - to name but a few.

The amount you should drink is a hotly debated subject, as there are many variables to consider including weight, height, age, physical activity, gender and your geographic location.

However, from my experience, an average person who is moderately active and with no underlying health issues relating to water or water consumption should aim to drink a minimum of two litres of water per day, aiming closer to three if possible.

All non-caffeinated and non-alcoholic drinks can be included in this figure, although I would dissuade you from drinking fruit juices, as these tend to contain high amounts of sugar.

In my opinion, the hydration gained from the water in the food you eat should be considered a bonus.

Why are caffeinated and alcoholic drinks to be excluded from your daily water consumption target? Caffeinated and alcoholic drinks work in the opposite way to water – these dehydrate you.

By inhibiting the release of ADH (Anti-Diuretic Hormone), caffeine and alcohol cause your kidneys to reabsorb less fluid and instead they produce more urine. That is not to say that a couple of coffees or the odd alcoholic drink is necessarily a problem, but excessive consumption can contribute to dehydration.

Here are two tips to help you increase your water intake:

- Carry water with you and you'll drink it. Have it available in your office and you'll drink it. It is simply a matter of developing a new and very worthwhile habit.

- Take a pint of water to bed with you and drink it immediately upon waking in the morning every day.

3. Only take antibiotics when necessary

One of my specialist fields of study is the improvement of digestive health, and how our gut bacteria (our microbiome) influences our overall health.

It is important to understand that antibiotics can be lifesavers and that I am not against their use if necessary.

However, antibiotics are designed to kill bacteria, and rarely discriminate between the *bad gut bacteria* causing the problem and your *good gut bacteria*.

Good gut bacterial cells outnumber our human cells by up to 10-1, and co-exist in a symbiotic relationship with us. They influence our physiological and psychological wellbeing, providing us with many benefits including support of our immune system, and producing importance hormones and vitamins. Given the importance the role of our good gut bacteria plays for our overall health, it makes sense to look after them.

Antibiotic resistance is becoming a significant global threat.

It is possible that if antibiotics are taken regularly, you could develop antibiotic resistant bacteria in your gut, leading to other serious issues.

In my view, if you are with your doctor and antibiotics are prescribed, then you should ask if they are necessary. It is always good to ask, as antibiotics are not the 'cure all' that some people believe them to be and their over-use can have implications.

If you take a course of antibiotics, it is good practice to follow up afterwards with a course of quality *probiotics* that includes a mix of Lactobacillus and Bifidobacterium strains and has a strength of at least 10billion *colony forming units (CFUs)*. These will help to repopulate your friendly bacteria and will help educe the chance of any remaining bad bacteria gaining a foothold in your gut.

There is not enough space here to scratch the surface of the topic of the link between good gut health and that of improved physical and mental wellbeing, but suffice to say that I am an advocate of taking daily probiotics.

4. Read food labels

Many people eat and drink with no real understanding of the nutrient breakdown or calories in what they consume. If you want to improve your energy levels and overall health, then you need to understand – and be accountable for – what goes in your mouth.

Learning to read food labels properly is a skill, but a thorough knowledge is not necessary for most people.

A good starting point for many is to understand the Government's *traffic light* system that is on most food packaging. *Red, Amber, Green* – it is that simple.

Whilst the traffic light system is not infallible by any means, it is certainly better than nothing.

Avoid the red, limit the amber and where possible go for the green - simple.

Once you start to use to the traffic light system regularly, then I recommend getting a deeper understanding of food labels, to enable you to interpret the full nutritional breakdown in the food you eat.

If you want to be truly accountable and control the nutritional/calorific breakdown of the foods you eat, then utilise a food diary. There are many Apps available on mobile devices. It might feel a little odd to begin with, and you needn't strive for perfection when recording what you eat, but get it right most of the time and it will be enlightening just how much (or how little) food you are eating and the calorific, carbohydrate, fat, protein, sugar and fibre breakdown of that food.

5. Get enough sleep

Poor quality or insufficient sleep can leave you exhausted, which has an impact on your thinking ability and performance. During periods of sufficient good quality sleep, your body goes through a process of repair, restoration and rejuvenation. Six to eight hours of sleep per night is considered adequate for most people.

If you have trouble sleeping, here are a few tips:

- **Have two kiwi fruits an hour before going to bed, every day.** Kiwi has potent anti-oxidant properties which help to boost the immune system, enhancing cell protection and repair. Kiwi is high in Serotonin – a hormone that acts as a neurotransmitter and which is the precursor to our 'sleep hormone', Melatonin. Serotonin is involved in a range of physiological and psychological processes, from digestion to cardiovascular functioning, from regulation of appetite to influencing your moods. Serotonin also helps to initiate sleep and is a significant factor in controlling the stages of sleep, including deep sleep.

- **Regulate your body's own natural body clock.**
  Be consistent with your sleep schedule both during
  the week and weekends.

- **Turn off blue-light emitting devices an hour before
  going to bed.** Research has found that blue-light
  emitting devices make you feel more alert and
  suppresses Melatonin levels - and you need Melatonin
  to get a decent night's sleep.

- **Avoid drinking caffeine after 4pm.**

- **Write down things that are on your mind,** as this
  process can help you relax.

6. Exercise regularly

There are benefits to regular exercise; it boosts energy
levels, helps to combat health conditions and illnesses
(including stroke, Type II Diabetes, Depression, Arthritis and
different types of Cancers) as well as helping to improve mood.

Whatever exercise you do, no matter how little, it is better
than doing nothing. Even walking for 30 minutes a day has its
benefits. So, set a goal to exercise every day. Your body (and
mind) will thank you for it.

Improved health and energy levels are within reach of
everyone. There are many more ways to improve your health
and energy levels than are outlined here, and should you wish
to contact me to discuss these, please visit:

www.i-nutrition.co.uk/contact

Realising the importance of optimal health, energy and
vitality both in your professional and personal life and finding
ways to improve is worth the effort.

Neil D'Silva a qualified nutritionist and founder of *i-Nutrition* and who specialises in helping professionals to improve their overall health, to lose weight safely and sustainably and to restore their energy levels. He also specialises in improving gut-related issues.

In addition to working with individual clients, i-Nutrition also offers support with overall weight management, childhood obesity, inflammatory bowel conditions, and also provides corporate employee wellbeing programmes.

Website	*www.i-nutrition.co.uk*
Facebook	*www.facebook.com/inutritionuk*
Twitter	*www.twitter.com/inutritionuk*
LinkedIn	*www.linkedin.com/in/neildsilva*

Feed Your Mind: 3 x 3 Mind Routines, Food Rituals and Recipes For Busy Leaders

Dom Mason

I want you to think like an ultra-runner. Close your eyes and imagine you are running 100 kilometres in one day. Now imagine you are 57 kilometres in.

How do you feel?

Now, I want you to think first of your stomach, and then your legs. Think of your stomach as a tiny bag through which all your water and energy must be taken in. This is all you can do to fuel the rest of your run. That bag (your stomach) can only hold so much volume and only process so much content per hour.

Now think of your legs muscles. Think of the amount of energy stored in your leg muscles, being burned by running and being renewed from your stomach.

Just think of your stomach and your leg muscles.

Now imagine everything else you could be doing.

Looking left and right, thinking hard about the route, swinging your arms, checking time, position, messages, breathing heavily, changing music tracks, chewing gum, holding a map ... think of some other things you could be doing until you have a mental list of everything else you could be doing. Got it?

Now be aware that all of that activity is not digesting food or absorbing water; it's not your legs running.

It's all wasted energy. Wasted effort.

When you run an ultra-marathon, everything you are doing is planned around digesting food, absorbing water and running (well, almost all but we'll come to that later). Why do you plan an ultra-marathon like that? Simple.

Energy + Productivity = Success

But, this isn't a lesson in how to run an ultra-marathon, this is just an example to help steer you. So, let's take that attitude of *reserving energy and maximising productivity* into your working life, your life as a leader, and let's see where it takes us. Given my demanding professional life this is what I do to maximise my energy.

1. Mind routines

Slow down
Business over *busy*-ness. Do people think someone who is always busy is in control? Do they approach that person and expect to have time with them in deep conversation? No.

Briefly revisiting ultra-runners, not everything they do is running. Do you honestly think they run the whole race? Most probably not, they pace themselves between running and fast walking to achieve their long distance goals. They walk steep ridges, they slow down for a period after food, they accept having to go slower through hazardous conditions.

You should not wish to appear chaotically busy. You want to appear serious but remain open and available to your staff. Try slowing down your meetings, pace, timbre and walking by 15% and see what effect it has on yourself and others.

Execute

A leader commits. Leaders that have routine and then make clear decisions, in public, perform best. As the world grows more complex and things move more quickly, a set of key routines should be the metronome and bedrock for how you work. However, as well as a cyclical, inclusive way of working, leaders need to execute in a practical way.

Execution gives a leader a method to understand their own performance and better understand where they can impact for future success. This understanding of your own capability to plan and execute will also aid colleagues. There are too many fossilised ways of working that magnify colleagues' view of leaders as false, bureaucratic and contributing little. Combat that cynicism with routines that best support successful execution.

Be Tribal

People are tribal. You have to navigate those tribes, as well as leading your own. Even in the largest organisations, people look to and take cues from the people around them. Conversely, even in the smallest functions, you will find intense, tribal behaviour. If you're going to have more effective change, if we are going to move from *imposing* to *inclusive* change, you have to learn to work with tribes and their influencers. Most change tries to leverage hierarchy to move work forwards and this requires us to identify the key influencers who will drive local uptake.

Leaders need to identify and include key influencers who will be affected by changes. You will then use these influencers to shape and drive the change and its implementation locally. This will require you to think tribally about how to include people in change. This ability to identify tribal influencers, and then use them to get traction on the ground, is a skill you should train.

2. Food Rituals

Regularity

Planned regular meals benefit you significantly. On average, we eat six times each day – breakfast, lunch and dinner and in-between snacks. And almost 33% of food is now being eaten outside of the home. And that trend is growing.

You are more likely to eat a balanced meal when you are in control of what, and how much, you put on your plate. As well as weight gain alone, eating regularly reduces insulin resistance. Regular meal eaters tend to have a lower energy (calorie) intake compared to those who eat irregularly for two reasons. We eat more overall and we tend towards energy rich snacks. Eating regular meals helps keep your blood sugar levels stable.

There are many food myths around regular mealtimes, for example:

"Food eaten in the evening is more fattening". An evening meal does not make the body store more fat compared to the same number of calories eaten at any other time of day. It's not the time food is eaten; it's the number of calories eaten.

"Lunch is for losers!" Lunch is for productive people who want to benefit from taking 20-45 minutes out to relax and refuel.

So how do you get the nutrition you need and avoid eating on the fly or falling into the snack trap? Two ways.

- **Plan ahead** If there is a day (or days) when you're always late home or you must eat at work, make sure you have the ingredients for a meal that is quick to cook and nutritious.

- **Cook in bulk.** The next time you make a meal that's easy to cook extra portions of, do so. This ensures that you always have a nutritious meal in the house ready for those 'I'm too tired to cook' days.

Sleep food

You need to eat for your sleeping hours. Your diet regulates your energy levels during the day, but many people forget the obvious fact that it also prepares your body for sleep.

As well as eating to fuel your days, eating the correct things prepares your body to function well when sleeping. This includes repair and recovery, regulating bodily functions such as hormone production, and important processes within organs and bones that can only happen during rest and sleep. Our immune system, many processes for healthy blood cells and normal brain and heart functions rely on sleep.

Food that aids processes that occur during sleep will help you perform all these functions. This needs to be healthy balance of proteins, carbohydrates and fats. It should be a varied diet to make a range of micronutrients - minerals, vitamins and antioxidants - available to your sleeping body.

To have the best food for sleep, seek out foods you like that contain: B vitamins, Calcium, Magnesium, Vitamin D, and Tryptophan-rich foods such as chicken, nuts and seeds.

Nothing is an option

Fasting is fine, at the right time. Limiting calorie intake is nothing new — it's a spiritual practice in many cultures and religions. But people also fast for health and other non-religious reasons, including to lose weight, to prepare for medical testing, to try to prevent aging, to detox, to boost immunity, and to overcome addictions.

If you're thinking about fasting for any reason, here are three tips that will help:

Try Different Tactics

For weight loss the key is to lose it slowly, as this allows you to maintain the greatest amount of muscle. Instead of going to extremes by fasting to lose weight rapidly, think about initially eliminating some (but not all) foods for a few weeks.

Pay attention to any trigger foods, or foods you find difficult to control portion-wise. Some people find that eliminating sugar can help them readjust their tastes and rediscover the natural sweetness in foods.

Another effective strategy is to focus on what you can have versus what you cannot have. Begin by setting a simple goal such as having one to two cups of vegetables as a meal only, and two to three servings of fruit each day.

Adapt Your Activities

With a significant change in your dietary intake, you'll have to consider what changes you'll need to make in your daily activities. This really depends on the type of fasting you're doing, but high intensity workouts may need to be delayed until your fasting period is over.

Plan What Meals You Do Take

Every fast should have a period during the day when you consume something, and the choices during that time should be balanced and nutritious. Think about starting with one to two glasses of water with a handful of dried fruit or nuts. The water, sugar, protein and micronutrients will help you quickly rebound from the fast. If you break a fast each day find well-rounded meals with whole grains, healthy lean protein, and plenty of vegetables to feed your hungry body.

With that in mind, take these recipes and mix, change and combine them into your favourites for a nutritious, flavour-packed day.

Recipes

I like to take recipes like these and mix, change and combine them into your favourites for a nutritious, flavour-packed day.

Petite Championne
French savoury oatmeal is a potent breakfast boost.

Cook the oats. Cook the egg (how you like it). Chop the other ingredients into the oats. Chop in the egg if you like or serve it on the side.

- 1/4 mug dry quick-cooking steel cut oats

- 2 tbsps shredded mozzarella or goats cheese

- 1 tsp coconut oil

- 1/4 cup diced red peppers

- 2 tbsps finely chopped onions

- 1 large egg

Beach Bean Curry
A spicy adventure for lunch.

Reserve the turmeric and curry powder and mix the rice and edamame with the other ingredients. Add the turmeric and curry slowly to your taste, they can be potent!

- 3 cups cooked brown rice, short grain

- 1 1/4 cups edamame beans, cooked

- Maple syrup or honey (to taste)

- 1 tbsp tahini

- 1 small red onion, finely chopped

- 1 lemon, juiced

- 1-2 tsp turmeric powder

- 2 tsp curry powder

- Cayenne and smoky paprika (to taste)

Mountain Balls
Super-powered pocket snacks.

Make the peanut butter. Stir all ingredients together, adding water carefully for texture. Refrigerate immediately but don't freeze.

- 1 mug natural peanut butter (just peanuts and pinch of salt in a blender)

- 1/4 mug honey

- 2 teaspoons vanilla extract

- 1 1/2 mugs rolled oats

- 1/2 mug unsweetened shredded coconut

- 1/3 mug chopped 90% cocoa chocolate

- 2 teaspoons water

I hope you find these mind routines, food rituals and recipes useful to aid your journey. It's been exciting to bring you these mindful, healthy and enriching tips to being a better leader.

Remember, take that attitude of *reserving energy and maximising productivity* through all of your life as a leader, and see where it takes you.

Dom Mason is a Digital Transformation consultant. He trains leaders who need to meet digital challenges head-on. He actively manages the journey to digital excellence.

He says: "As a leader, you know that the technology in every part of your business is constantly shifting. Your customers' needs are driving change, opening new threats, but also creating new opportunities if you can take them. Transformation needed won't happen by itself, and my expertise can save you time and huge expense."

LinkedIn   *www.linkedin.com/in/dominic-mason-70a4ab/*

Acknowledgment

Emily, thanks for giving me some small insight into your knowledge of food, health and mindfulness. This chapter is testament to your energy. Thanks also for sharing your amazing journey with me.

Santé passe richesse.

Movement as the Centrepiece

Elizabeth Banks

As a child I loved nothing more than being able to ride my bike, kick a football around, chase my friends, climb stuff, jump off stuff, and roll downhill. What I wasn't thinking about was whether my body would allow me to do it. I was only concerned about being the fastest, climbing a tree or keeping playing around on my skateboard.

I naturally had a big *Movement Bank* where I made daily investments and opened multiple accounts.

As someone who tries to not have regrets my only disappointment now is that I didn't keep up with my payments along the way. I do find myself thinking what if I hadn't stopped running, jumping and climbing the way that I did as a kid; fearless, thoughtless, relentless - what would my account balance be now?

Our ability to move is fundamentally linked to every aspect of our day. I believe there is no greater increase to performance than to improve our capacity, quality and frequency of movement.

Do You Take Amex? The Movement Bank

Movement has many different currencies with which we can invest in our *Movement Bank*.

Some of us use the currency of yoga, some the currency of *CrossFit,* some use the gym, some invest in spinning, some utilize walking the dog, and some of us have been spending too much and not investing much at all lately!

To bring us to a common language I'm going to talk about your *Movement Bank.* We all pretty much have a bank account and we understand the necessity to make payments into that account so that we can buy things (essential and non-essential) for all that life offers. If you make regular payments you have a *healthy account* – it's in credit. The months that you spent over what you paid-in you are in your overdraft, in the red and likely incurring hefty charges. Our *Movement Bank* isn't so different. In the months and years when we are engaging in frequent, quality movement, we build ourselves a credit in our bodies and in our overall health; and in the times when we overspend, neglecting or depleting our physical health – often trading it for other goods or rewards – we incur a debt to our health and physical livelihood.

What's In Store?

Let's have a quick look at where we're at, and what is happening in the health arena currently. We'll cut through the noise. The focal point in this chapter is capacity. We need to understand how and why movement influences our capacity and therefore our ability to be *Fit for Purpose.*

We'll take a quick journey into the brain and see why current thinking in neuroscience needs to be included in the process. Lastly, we'll discuss some considerations that affect your movement quality and essential ways to grow your *Movement Bank.*

Just Tell Me

I see clients confused by rapidly changing and conflicting advice. I also see a shift in the wellness arena with people taking more interest and ownership for their health supported by technology that delivers real time information and autonomy.

Who's In Charge? The Brain is the Governor

Have you thought about why we have a brain? Your first thought might be, *To be alive*, which is true, but isn't the whole picture. Plants are alive, but don't have a nervous system, as they are not mobile. *We have a brain so we can move.*

The connection between our brain and movement was best explained to me by the story of the humble sea squirt (Ascidiacea). This little guy swims around the sea, looking for his perfect place to set up camp. Once he's found the perfect rock to attach himself to for the rest of his life, he proceeds to eat his own brain. Doesn't need to move, so he doesn't need a brain. For a far more elegant version of this story have a look at Daniel Wolpert's *TEDTalk: The Real Reason for Brains.*

What this tells us is that if the brain is built to make movement possible, then we need to practice that movement – in high quality and high frequency repetition – to create the healthiest brain possible. That is going to be the key to dealing with stress, life's struggles, the daily juggle, and those times when we have to debit the account more than we'd like.

Why The Size Of Your Bank Account Matters: Invest in Your Health For Your Future Self

In becoming *Fit for Purpose* there are many different elements to consider, but I want us to specifically focus on health. It is likely that we will all have a somewhat different definition of what healthy is, but for me it really comes down to capacity.

When there is money in the account, we know that we can pay our bills on time, we have options to do stuff, to purchase kit, invest in software and people, or to take holidays; we have capacity.

Without money in the account we have no capacity and everything grinds to a halt. In the corporate arena, we are in pursuit of the best version of ourselves, if you have no capacity you will fall short of that goal.

Don't sacrifice what you want right now
for what you really want

One of the challenges we face is planning for the longer-term. We are all familiar with the feeling of wanting something, and maybe it's something we've wanted for a long time.

Many times, our purchases are not vital in the short-term. What happens is we convince ourselves that our short-term desires are congruent with our long-term vision.

Our brains are not very adept at projecting into the future financially or in relation to our health. It's why it's easier to make regular withdrawals from the account in terms of alcohol, smoking, junk food, poor movement patterns, and late nights. We're not thinking about the bigger impact in those moments. Have you found yourself thinking, *"That won't happen to me"* when seeing older people become less mobile or sick?

It is time to change that belief. If the account isn't topped up, it certainly *could* happen to you.

I believe that health sits at the core of all areas of life. It is the red
thread that connects all that we do.

Help, I'm Overdrawn! Getting Back in the Black

Can you recall the last time you felt vulnerable? It was probably something quite significant.

I'm not talking about just lacking confidence, but a time that you actually felt endangered. You probably felt a mild sense of panic, or anxiety, and began to lean toward the *fight or flight* response that's in all of us.

Because we start thinking about protecting ourselves and getting out of the situation, it's pretty straightforward for us to understand that this will have a huge influence on our ability to function at a high level.

What's not so apparent is that our brain is hard-wired for our survival and is continually monitoring and assessing threats to us. It does this so at any time, when a threat is perceived, it is ready to respond and keep us safe.

Think about having all the *Apps* on your phone open and wanting to play a video to be met with the *wheel of frustration* as your phone tries to process the task.

Having the survival responses of our brain stay active is a lot like having that wheel spinning on the phone. You just can't accomplish what you want to get done.

Sometimes you must hard-close *Apps* to create some processing power so there's enough available to do what you want. In our health, sometimes we have to cut out some draining activities – or dangerous activities – to allow the stress and survival systems to reset.

Let's take it a layer deeper and look at what is draining your account, specifically your brain and nervous system.

In simple terms, the nervous system has three parts: *sympathetic*, which is often described as our *fight or flight* response, *parasympathetic,* referred to as *rest and digest*, and our *autonomic nervous system* that regulates bodily functions below our level of awareness.

The *sympathetic nervous system* is not simply protecting us from the bear or lion that may attack us like we were cavemen, but in our modern world it serves us in other intricate ways.

It can notice and shield us from a car coming from the edge of our vision, or move quickly to protect our physical body when a loud *BANG!* is heard behind us. This is the program that runs in the background, consistently, tirelessly and thoroughly.

It can also detect mismatch in our sensory systems, which could be threatening if we can't understand what's going on around us.

We are walking beings, we navigate the world with our eyes, looking around our environment. This visual information must be integrated accurately with our balance system, which tells us which way is up.

Both must be integrated with our body posture and position that is being reported to our *proprioceptive system*.

If the sensory signals don't match, or the brain can't integrate them, then the *sympathetic nervous system* kicks into high gear to start protecting us from something that *might* be dangerous in the environment.

As we go about our day our brain is *receiving* information through these systems, *interpreting* vast amounts of information and then *deciding* what action to take.

High quality inputs will *add* to your account, and crappy inputs will *drain* your account, because for every moment the system is protecting you it's not investing good quality movement into your future health.

Have a lot of documents to read, so you spend hours looking at a computer screen? If your visual input is poor this will be a high cost on your account. Back bugging you by the end of the day?

Our eyes and our balance system are intrinsically linked to our spine, and the muscles that create quality posture. Having a problem in one of these systems could be an on-going debit to your account.

I see lots of people professionally who are in some level of pain. If you have been unfortunate enough to experience back pain you will know first-hand what a huge drain on your capacity this is. Pain is a first-class bank robber when it comes to stealing capacity from your account.

Injuries are all too frequent; if your account is hovering just in the black you risk being one workout away from ending up in the red, resulting in 'pulling a muscle' or flaring up that old injury. Bottom line – that one small mistake could create a serious dip in performance.

Staying healthy and well is just as important as getting healthy and well.

My Accounts are Leaking!
Dealing With Pain and Other Capacity Drains

Pain is a complex topic, but I want to touch on a few key points that may help you if you are currently experiencing pain. The fact is, understanding how pain works can lower your experience of pain. Knowledge is power.

Our brain is able to process more accurately when we know what's going on, rather than jumping to worst-case scenario thinking. One such bit of knowledge is that the level of pain is not descriptive to the level of tissue damage. Think about when you get a paper cut – it's incredibly painful for such a small cut. But it's not a severe injury. But if we don't understand this, then the on-going pain can make us think we're in much greater danger than we really are.

Pain isn't the only thing leaking money from your account, there are a myriad of other factors as well. How well we see, balance, breathe, and sleep, our hydration levels, nutrition, mind-set, stress levels, fun factor, and our history of injuries, can all create leaks of their own.

Growing a Healthy Account

With so many potential leaks and debits, it's going to take a lot of credits to the account to keep us flush. When looking to add *credits* to your account it's wise to cover all the bases, so take a review of where each of those areas are currently.

We're not looking for perfection in every area, just thinking about how we could be better.

Start with success; what can I do this week? *"This week I can prioritise my sleep by getting to bed 30 minutes earlier or removing electronics from my bedroom."* Consider wearing blue-blocker glasses for evening screen time. They minimise the blue-light load that wreaks havoc on our hormonal and circadian rhythms. Spend time in nature; forest bathing is proven to shrink stress, to enhance our immune system, to reduce heart rate and blood pressure as well as improve overall feelings of wellbeing. Walk barefoot on the grass, take your eyes for a workout by looking far into the distance. These add huge value to your account without being task driven.

Keep in mind, high quality movement is the biggest, most frequent, and most valuable investment that we can make.

The Bottom Line

Adult life, filled with adult-sized problems, can seem like the direct debit you keep forgetting to cancel, slowly stealing your hard-earned cash. If we allow it.

As a leader with a responsibility to look after your people, committing to daily investments in your health will filter through to all areas of your life. Make sure your account is in credit, a future in the red needn't become the default.

We have the opportunity to utilise the exciting new world of neuroscience to improve our health and performance in a way that has never been more accessible to all.

Invest in your health for your future self

Start Right NOW! My Favourite Drill

One of my favourite drills is what I call the *energy ball drill*. Try it with me.

First I imagine I have an *energy ball* swirling between my hands. I start the drill by moving my hands through circular and spiral motions together, as if I was running them over the seams of a basketball.

As I keep the ball *alive* by being in constant motion, I start to move the rest of my body so I can pass the ball around my trunk, overhead, bring it close to me, stretch it away from me, swoop it close to the ground. I focus on the swirl of the ball in a smooth and rhythmic manner.

I visualise the ball shrinking and growing, as if it were the size of a tennis ball, and then growing to be a beach ball.

The ball has my total focus. I am only aware of my breath and heartbeat, and the rhythm of my movement. Sometimes I move across the surface pretending to take ninja-like steps, sometimes I keep feet firmly planted in the grass. It can be for just a few minutes or it can just be for 45 seconds.

The *energy ball drill* creates a multitude of movements, enriches the body map, lowers the alarm systems and increases capacity. I sharpen my focus and generate energy for my day. All with my body and no kit required.

Money in the bank!

Elizabeth Banks is the founder of *The Movement Bank* and a movement specialist with over 18 years' experience in the health and fitness industry.

She helps people with injuries return to what they love to do. She works with clients including urban and professional athletes in a studio and clinical setting. Her assessment is done via a neurological lens to calibrate the body's systems to regain full function.

Elizabeth is qualified in Sport Science and has certifications with the *Gray Institute of Functional Science, Z-Health* and *AMN Academy* with a focus on movement neurology, biomechanics, fascial work, foot mobilisation, mindset coaching and behavioural change.

Email   *e@themovementbank.com*

Web   *www. themovementbank.com*

References

- AMN Academy: Calibrate course manual

- Cobb. E.W: Zhealth, 9S Structure certification manual

- Cobb. E.W: Zhealth, 9S The Next Evolution certification manual

- Doidge, N. *The Brain's Way of Healing.* 2016. Penguin Books

- Dr David S. Butler. *The Sensitive Nervous System.* 200. Noigroup Publications

- Llinás. R Rodolpho. *I of the Vortex. From Neurons to self.* 2002. MIT Press

- Sandra Blakeslee & Matthew Blakeslee. *The Body Has A Mind Of It's Own.* 2008. Random House

- *Effect of phytoncide from trees on human natural killer cell function.* DOI: 10.1177/039463200902200410

- Daniel Wolpert TED Talk: *The real reason for brains:* https://www.ted.com/talks/daniel_wolpert_the_real_reason_for_brains#t-93628

Building The Foundations of Failure

Sarah-Anne Lucas

And so it begins, our quest into the truth of you as a leader. Come take my hand and together we will test your potential.

You see leadership begins and ends with you. Your loves, your losses, your values and beliefs. What you know to be true and having the courage to die by your sword. Your daily behaviour, your ability to relate and build connections and love people more than they love you.

This is where your quest begins, moving into the truth of you.

I am cursed with telling you the truth: *What I believe to be true.* I am not saying you are lying, but you are not telling the truth to yourself.

I have been blessed with having the greatest teacher in communication, my eldest son Jack. Jack has taught me to be prescriptive with my language. If not, then the outcome will not be the one desired.

Jack is autistic. If you do not honour and respect the power of language with him, then prepare for the wrath of Jack to fall upon you. Jack has the most powerful and painful meltdowns. He is aggressive to inanimate objects, such as wardrobes, walls and many a door has been beaten to an inch of it's life.

But, on request Jack would always take his meltdown to his room. His school which supported his needs taught him the skill of self soothing. Within his room and having time as a contributing factor Jack would come down from a 10 to a 4 on the Richter scale.

On one occasion, I gave Jack time and space to heal and went to offer a loving hand. He was not reaching back to me. I asked Jack, *"My darling don't you trust Mumma a hundred percent?"*

"No I do not!"

Oh my days, this was like a dagger going straight into my soul and then an extra twist for luck. Can you imagine your son not trusting you?

Jack proceeded to laugh in my face. Here come-outh the lesson:

"Mumma, if only you had said do I trust you, I would have answered yes. But you had to add the hundred percent"

Conscious, precise, prescriptive language was born.

I deliberately practice words to be visceral. For you to feel them in your nervous system. For the words to be injected into every cell of your body. For you to feel the power of the word. Enjoy!

You see, you and I hear watered down messages everyday about leadership, how to be a great leader and the systems and processes to create an amazing business.

On trend phrases of: making people feel safe, build connections it's all about collaboration, failure is learning and my favourite is building resilience in your business.

If you believe leadership of people is how to create and grow a business, you are missing the point. To be a leader of people can only come from an awareness and understanding of leading oneself *everyday*.

Leading oneself is building the body of your business, YOU.

What you do on a daily basis creates the body you find yourself in today. If you are not able to lead yourself, why should others have faith in your leadership skills.

You have to show them, not tell them.

You are being watched constantly. How you move, what you wear, the tone of your voice, the food you eat and the words you choose to speak. *They* are watching. *Show, don't tell.*

But I meet and hear from leaders, experts in their field who feel exhausted, fat, unfit, nothing left to give. Their relationships are failing, with their partner, their children and their friends. They have little connection with themselves let alone anyone else. They are holding on to the ideology that they are building a business for their family. The family that they are failing to lead. Harsh, but true.

They employ reasons of time or lack of energy to not invest in themselves. They can't wait to spend their time on holiday with the failing family that they hate spending time with.

Regardless of this feedback, their millionaire mindset continues to fool them into building the business for their family.

Before this millionaire, this leader can change, collapse is their only saviour. Collapse is the only catalyst for this leader to inject new behaviour. This is where building the foundations of failure will lead you to thrive.

Are you ready to fail? Are you willing to put yourself out there?

To take to the stage and fail in front of your audience, a live one at that? Are you willing to practice your performance and perform your practice? Remember: *show, don't tell.*

Are you willing to go into the depths of your thoughts? Are you willing to move into the fear of pain? True fear, to the death fear. Are you willing to ask one of the greatest questions: *What do I believe?*

Build the body of your business on the foundations of failure. We hear constantly that failures are where we grow. Without the suffering and pain you have endured throughout your life your mastery of resilience is extinct. Everyday, regardless, no matter you are going to build the body of your business. Regardless, no matter what!

Without you there is no business.

Without you there is no vision.

Without you there is no leadership.

When I speak around the globe I always ask two questions.

I ask the audience to hear the first question, and if this is what they believe I ask them to stand up, but, if they stand up they are then eliminated from answering the second question.

Question 1: Do you believe that health is a *choice?*

Yes or No? If you answered *Yes*, you are excluded from answering the second question.

Question 2: Or, do you believe that health is your *duty?*

Breath in these questions.

I believe that health is your *duty*, not your *choice*. When did health become a choice? Total no-sense. I believe it is your duty, everyday, regardless, no matter what, to support, love and guide your body into health. Health is your duty, not your choice. How rude of you to not love your body!

If you believe you're a leader, then when did you decide that you do not have time or energy to put health into your body? It does not make sense. *Show, don't tell.*

Leading yourself, leading your family, leading your business and leading your community begins and ends with you. How you think and feel, how you move and grow, and how you behave.

Health, nutrition, movement, behaviour are all part of testing your potential as a leader. As a leader you must think like the people you want to impact.

Health, energy, peak performance is simple but not easy. Peak performance has three vital requirements from you.

- Unwavering faith
- Intensity
- Consistency

What you do on a *daily* basis gives you the body you find yourself with, right at this moment. Here are the three simplest of daily rituals that create the greatest impact on your energy.

- Drink water
- Cold showers
- Electronic sundown

To help you go deeper into your health I have created many daily rituals that you can test in your life. The idea is to find the rituals that are just right for you. Remember it's the relationship you have with yourself that is the greatest gift. Listen to the body, it is genius. If it is not having a profound effect, *adapt* to another ritual. But test, test and test again.

- You know your body
- You have had it all your life
- Listen to it, and adjust

An incredible billionaire client always shares his business wisdom: *Adjust, keep adjusting and with speed.* This drives his fellows crazy, nevertheless he continues to adjust creating the most miraculous results. If your body is not responding, adjust.

Here are three daily rituals for you to test that will deliver remarkable positive results.

Daily Ritual 1 for Peak Performance:
Drink beautiful quality water

Look at the words I use, beautiful quality water. It matters the thoughts and feelings you have when performing this ritual.

Every morning before anything goes into the body, drink 500mls of water. Super simple. Add a slice of lemon or lime to taste.

Drinking beautiful quality water should then continue throughout your day. The health authorities recommend 8 x glasses (8 ounce glasses) or 1800-2000mls per day.

90% of my clients all say they do not drink enough water. Some only have water as part of the tea/coffee process. If you are one of the masses who don't drink enough water, now is the time to create radical change. Water is the most wonderful source of energy. Without it you would not exist.

It matters the quality of the water. Tap water in the UK is not of the purest quality. The toxins and hormones found in tap water can block the energy efficiency of the cells. You are creating peak performance within each of your *estimated* 63 trillion cells in your body.

There are many options for producing quality water in your home from built-in water filter systems to advanced water filter systems that sit elegantly on your kitchen side that will provide the highest quality water for your family. Research a water filter system that is right for you and your family. But drink quality water.

Action

First thing, drink 500mls beautiful quality water. Eight glasses a day. Add lemon or lime to taste. Keep the practice simple. Drink beautiful quality water. Everyday, regardless.

I always carry a bottle of home filtered water with me. If you don't carry a bottle with you, you can bet you are dehydrated. Not adequately hydrated will compromise the performance of your energy system.

Please carry water with you, sip throughout the day and importantly, love every moment taken hydrating your body. You are shifting your energy system into peak performance.

Daily Ritual 2 for Peak Performance: Cold Showers - Cold Thermogenesis

This is a super simple daily ritual that causes the most resistance. The pattern that is emerging, women more than men have a huge challenge with this ritual.

The cold water shocks the cell. It creates adaptation in the powerhouse of the cell. Otherwise known as *Mitochondria Metabolism*. But the benefits are ridiculous:

- Stimulate weight loss
- Increase Testosterone levels in men
- Increase fertility
- Improve hair and skin health
- Improve immunity
- Improve circulation
- Increase muscle recovery… for all you athletes
- Energise the breath - use *The Box Breathing* technique
- Regulation of emotions
- Increase alertness
- Mitochondria metabolism

Action

Begin with 15 seconds. As cold as you can go for 15 seconds, after your normal shower. Test:

- 2 days of 15 seconds
- 2 days of 30 seconds
- 2 days of 45 seconds
- 2 days of 60 seconds

In a seven day cycle omit for one day. Take the day off from the cold. When showering, the breath is the essence of the ritual. Use *The Box Breathing Method*.

- Breath in for the count of four
- Hold the breath for the count of four
- Breath out for the count of four
- Hold the breath for the count of four

The ability to control the breath is the gateway to life. Invest 31 days into this practice. By day 20 you will feel energy like never before. Once you start you will never stop.

Daily Ritual 3 for Peak Performance:
Electronic Sundown

Super simple. No electronic equipment 90-minutes before retiring to sleep. The hormone, *Melatonin* is suppressed by electronic equipment: phones, tablets, hand-held devices.

If you can, no television. Read a book, meditate, rest, catch up with loved ones, prepare for tomorrow, write your gratitude journal. You will never run out of things to do. You are an incredible resourceful being.

Create a cave-like effect in your bedroom. Dark blackout curtains therefore no stimulus. No mobile phones. No TV.

Sleep is where recovery and repair occur. You are manipulating hormones to create the highest quality of sleep. Hormones such as testosterone and growth hormone peak within the hours of 2300-0300. The benefit is you wake up repaired, recovered and bursting with energy.

These rituals create the foundation for peak performance in the body. You will discover that actioning these three rituals, everyday, regardless, no matter what, will enhance your capacity to develop and grow without limits.

For best results, document the results you experience from these simple daily rituals. Witness what happens to you and witness the effect you create on the people around you.

Show, don't tell.

One thing you need to know. You maybe questioned as to why you are doing such ridiculous rituals. You may be ridiculed as to why you need peak performance. You may be condemned to isolation for your crazy behaviour.

Remain consistent. Remain wise. Remain strong in your faith.

In my experience your family, friends and community after battling their resistance will follow your lead. Know this to be true.

Expect set backs. You may encounter resistance. You will battle your intentions. But lean into the commitment needed o action these simple daily rituals.

But if you are the leader I know you to be, you will return to practice time and time again.

Continuing the quest to living an extraordinary life.

Sarah-anne Lucas aka *Bird*, is *Mumma* to three extraordinary *big* people.

She is also the founder of *Birdonabike*, the author of *It's Never About The Fitness*, podcaster, radio-host presenter, award winning businesswoman, global woman influencer, international speaker; qualified A&E nurse and Ironman.

Bird presents a weekly, live-to-air, guest interview radio show called *The Conversation* which is also available via download, *Podcast, iTunes* and *Soundcloud*.

She lives and breaths supporting you to believe in the health of your life. By using simple daily tweaks and biohacking, she helps busy, professionals achieve peak performance in health and life.

Bird's new book, *If That's What You Choose To Believe* promises *to* hold *you* accountable to be the most important person you know!

Web   *www.birdonabike.co.uk*

Mindset

Psychology, motivation, development, experience, upbringing, self-talk, emotions, feelings, resilience, emotional intelligence, self-worth, perceived ability to control, mental health

Notes on Emotionally Intelligent Leadership From The EQ Commando

Sean Foley

You can't get away from it!

In politics, business or banking, leaders in all walks of life are under extreme pressure to make great decisions and frankly, they are letting us down. Now more than ever we need authentic, trustworthy leadership we can engage with and depend on.

What does it really take to become the authentic, trusted leader who makes decisions that will benefit the many not the few?

I believe it boils down to emotions and the effect they have on us all.

Emotions are important for great leadership. Unchecked and unregulated though, they can destroy a leader's impact and influence, and worse still, they get people killed.

Join me to discover the most effective way to regulate your emotions to become an emotionally intelligent leader.

The leader we all wish we had!

The Pause:
When It Hits The Fan, Outstanding Leaders Don't React, They Pause And Breathe

My introduction to what I later learned was *Emotional Intelligence* or *EQ* was many years ago when I saw a lifesaving example of high *EQ* in action, in the form of a *pause*.

I was a *Royal Marines Commando* and for a time I was part of the *OC's Group* – the operational support team for the officer commanding a company of Marines.

In the midst of a *VUCA* environment *(Volatile, Uncertain, Confusing, Ambiguous)* our leader demonstrated excellent *Emotional Intelligence*, creating the environment for understanding and clear decision making - followed by precision execution - *to get us out of the sh*t.*

We were operational somewhere hot and it had hit the fan big time! With bullets flying, most people would expect him to *lead from the front* as an example to his team. He did exactly the opposite, achieving outstanding results. His immediate action was to hand over to his second (a young officer or Sergeant with combat experience, who would handle priority one: co-ordinating the troop's firepower to get and keep the enemy's heads down.)

The boss called his *Combat Response Team (CRT)* together and took a physical, mental and emotional step back so he could let the adrenaline subside and gather his thoughts.

The physical step back was to find cover, taking his *CRT* with him. Here he would not be interrupted by the madness taking place all around. As soon as we had dived into cover, he did something I didn't expect. *He paused.* He sat perfectly still, closed his eyes and took a deep breath.

Now I'm thinking *"This is no time to sleep! Take action, do leadership sh*t and help the lads"*. Time stood still, chaos erupting, he calmly took another deep breath!

Turns out he wasn't doing *nothing*. He explained to me later something I would never forget, he was - for a few seconds - choosing to *pause* and breathe.

Taking a mental and emotional step back - forcing ourselves to pause and breathe - allows information to travel from our emotional brain to our rationalising neocortex. This lets the fear response *(fight/flight/freeze)* pass, allowing the rational brain to take over, calmly process the situation and look for solutions.

This *pause* is vital for any leader to calmly process the facts and decide on effective action. This is best done away from the fray and doesn't take as long as most people think.

The *pause* consists of stopping what you are doing, becoming still and taking a deep breath or two making sure oxygen gets around the body to feed the brain. One of the reactions to fear can be to suspend breathing and when we do, our body starts to panic.

In panic mode we can't think rationally.

Military leaders have to be able to make the right decisions quickly and effectively under intense pressure or someone on their team's going to die.

In battle the leaders must sometimes remove themselves from the immediacy of the action and overwhelming emotions, process the facts, prioritise the issues and decide on the best course of action to support their troops.

Emotions play a vital part in leadership and they support you best when they are clearly identified, regulated and focussed towards understanding the challenge at hand to create outstanding results.

He surprised me again by taking out his notebook/aide-mémoire, so in the chaos he didn't miss a critical step in the effective response process he had started.

No matter how well you think you know a process, when it all goes pear shaped and emotions are surging it becomes really easy to miss a critical detail. Always have your simple step-by-step process written down so it's easy to follow.

Safely in cover with his team, his mind and emotions clear, regulated and relaxed, he used his experienced confidantes to help him evaluate the problem, assess resources available, decide on a plan and mobilise the right assets as quickly as possible.

His team were now communication Gods! Information, observations, recommendations were exchanged. His plan was quickly and effectively shared with key players by radio or satellite comms, everything clearly acknowledged.

When the challenge is understood, having a small group of experienced confidantes and specialist assets on hand helps a leader to clearly decide on and accurately direct necessary resources in the most effective way.

The tide was about to turn!

With support on its way, we re-joined the troops and the boss resumed command. Within a few minutes support arrived and we achieved his objective with minimal casualties.

What our leader did that day was save lives by pausing to identify and regulate his emotions, allowing his rational brain time to kick in. In *The Royal Marines* this contributes to what we call the *Commando Mindset*.

From *The Battlefield to The Boardroom*, developing a *Commando Mindset* will help you become the kind of leader others trust!

The Commando Mindset:
Do Not Allow Your Emotional Response To Dictate Your Immediate Action.

In high stress military environments, operators must be able to separate their emotional responses from their actions.

The *Marines* refer to this state of mind as *The Commando Mindset*. It helps to prevent knee jerk reactions that cost lives.

In a business environment, the stakes may not be so high, but the effects of mismanaged, emotionally driven reactions – or low emotional intelligence – can be devastating to company growth. You can't avoid emotions; they're part of your survival programming. As your brain constantly scans for danger, emotions will be triggered.

When your ancestors saw a tiger, they would feel fear which would make them take action to fight or run. The same program still runs today: whenever you think you're threatened, as in the story above, your brain sends out alert signals triggering action. Useful when there's a tiger or bullets are flying, not so much when you are in an argument with someone in the office!

Your default responses when you are fearful, frustrated or angry are not very effective in securing cooperation from other people but then your survival or chimp brain doesn't really care about that, it only cares about fulfilling your primary human need, to stay safe. So emotions are extremely useful for telling us when our own primary human need for safety is being met or not, but they're useless at helping us make rational operational, tactical or strategic decisions.

Consider this scenario.

You are the lead on a particularly challenging job that needs to be completed within a tight deadline.

You explain the challenge to a team mate and their response is less respectful than you would have liked.

You don't like their tone, language or implications. You feel irritated and defensive so you snap at them, to which they have a negative emotional response. They get defensive and react and off you both go, in a downward spiral into an argument or conflict. So now because of both of your interpretations, thoughts and emotional responses, two people aren't getting their primary need for safety met! At this point, your original aim has switched to a less productive one of winning this conflict.

To get the best results in any endeavour with other humans, you need create a culture of mutual respect that underpins the values of cooperation, collaboration and commitment.

Being able to effectively manage your emotional responses (developing emotional intelligence) is crucial to establishing these values in a team. If you feel yourself becoming fearful, frustrated or angry, you *must* pause and breathe *before* you respond or you run the risk of having a knee-jerk reaction and saying something that alienates, upsets or disengages others and they won't want to co-operate, collaborate or commit!

Now let's be clear, emotion is not the problem, the problem is your unregulated emotion that drives your default reaction – your unconscious response – that happens in a split second when you initially feel that surge of emotion. By becoming aware early of how you are feeling and building in a *pause*, you give yourself options and the opportunity to choose your response that will help to get the best outcome for everyone involved.

A *Commando Mindset* is rooted firmly in developing high *EQ Leadership* which positively influences teams, and filters through the company to create a culture of trust, respect and collaboration where people easily commit to achieving outstanding results.

While there's much more to high *EQ Leadership* than just a little pause and a *Commando Mindset,* it's a great place to begin to master what is arguably the number one resource in any situation.

Know Thy Self:
The No1 Resource In High EQ Leadership Is Self-Awareness

When you truly know yourself, you are well on your way to becoming the kind of outstanding leader you wish you'd had!

What does it mean to *know thyself* or be *self-aware*?

It's all about emotions. The good, the bad and the ugly! When you can accurately identify your emotions in any given moment, embrace and understand them and then regulate them to create more impact and influence in yourself and others, you are mastering the ageless challenge of knowing thyself.

My belief is that the most important assets in any endeavour are you, your people and your influence.

So outstanding leadership must start with being able to influence and lead yourself before you can influence and lead others. Emotional intelligence is the key to your ability to influence anyone.

As Daniel Goleman writes in *Emotional Intelligence: Why It Can Matter More Than IQ (1995)*, *self-awareness* is the first of the EQ competencies. By knowing yourself, you can manage your own emotions and thus control any actions you decide to take.

According to Goleman, there are five key competencies in emotional intelligence.

- **Self-Awareness** – Knowing your emotions.
- **Self-Regulation** – Managing your emotions.
- **Motivation** – Your inner drive.
- **Empathy** – Recognise and know others' emotions.
- **Social Skill** – Managing the emotions of others.

Of them, *self-awareness* is recognised as the single biggest step on the road to becoming an *Emotionally Intelligent Outstanding Leader.*

Self-Awareness

The most compelling, trusted and respected leaders are aware of their emotions and regulate them, giving them the advantage of being able to choose how to manage themselves; expertly deciding on the most appropriate responses and actions in every situation.

One of my favourite quotes that underpins this comes from Andrew Carnegie.

"The man (woman) who takes full possession of their own mind may take possession of anything else to which they are justly entitled."

Carnegie understood the power of self-awareness and self-regulation for more impact and influence in the world. Emotional intelligence is the key to knowing yourself, connecting with and positively influencing others and Carnegie became the richest man of his time by positively influencing his people.

Research carried out by the *Carnegie Institute of Technology* shows that *85% of your financial success is due to skills in human engineering, your personality and ability to communicate, negotiate, and lead or in other words, EQ. Shockingly, only 15 percent is due to technical knowledge.*

Self-awareness is the foundation for strong, charismatic leadership. Being highly self-aware allows leaders to engage their teams with openness and authenticity, powerfully guiding and empowering people to grow, develop and achieve more. What leader wouldn't want that?

Try this simple three-step process that will help you develop your self-awareness.

- **Step 1: Notice.** Become conscious of what's going on inside right now: the thoughts and emotions you are experiencing. For most people, emotions are easier to notice than thoughts. Tune into your body and become aware of what sensations are present.
  Now deliberately think of someone you love, noticing the emotional response in your body.
  Next, think of someone you don't like.
  Notice the new emotions and where you feel them.

- **Step 2: Name the emotions you're experiencing.** There are many emotions, for now I'll keep to basics: *Fear, Anger, Sadness, Happiness, Disgust, Shame.*

- **Step 3: Thought Triggers.** Identify the thought that triggered the emotion. Thoughts move very quickly, it can be hard to catch them. Notice when your thoughts are judging, name-calling or blaming someone else. When you catch yourself using one of these three, stop immediately. Actively choose to think a different thought about that person. Notice how you can change your emotion.

You can change what you feel by changing your thoughts – you're in control!

For example, if you catch yourself thinking, *"Simon is such an idiot",* you might feel angry, irritated or exasperated. If you then change how you word the thought such as, *"I don't like it when Simon does that"* you won't feel such a strong emotional response; you'll be calmer, more able to respond in a way that gets you what you really want.

Allocate ten minutes daily to sit quietly, simply notice what your body feels like. Observe your breathing.

Notice your thoughts and the emotions they generate. Are your thoughts mostly positive (producing enjoyable emotions) or mostly negative (producing unpleasant emotions)? Don't judge or evaluate, just observe.

Your *self-awareness* will develop with daily practice.

Whether you are on the battlefield or in the boardroom remember, in order to have more impact and influence with yourself and others, you must master the art of knowing yourself to lead yourself.

Develop your emotional intelligence to positively influence others and when it hits the fan, take a physical, mental and emotional step back, *pause,* breathe and regulate your emotions giving yourself the best chance of choosing the most effective actions!

Your team will love you for it and your business will thrive in these *VUCA* times!

References

- Goleman Daniel. (1995). *Emotional Intelligence: Why It Can Matter More Than IQ.* Bantam Books.
- Carnegie Andrew. 1835-1919. Quote.

Sean Foley believes, "The most important assets in any endeavour are: *You, Your People, Your Influence.* Emotional Intelligence is your influence".

Sean, *The EQ Commando* develops managers into leaders others would follow to battle.

He brings a unique blend of military and business leadership, behavioural profiling and extreme experiential learning to develop high emotional intelligence and resilience in leaders and managers who want to achieve their best.

He is a dedicated leadership trainer with 30 years of experience forged from combat operations with *The Royal Marines*, third world expeditions and leadership development for blue chips and SMEs. His passion for helping others succeed in extreme environments underpins his ability to engage and empower leaders to get outstanding results every time.

Sean has delivered fast, effective results around the globe in defence, O&G, finance, hospitality and education.

Whether your team is under fire or under-performing *The EQ Commando* helps you eliminate negatives, maximise positives, and accelerate results.

Phone	*0800 206 1916 Free*
Email	*sean@eq2lead.uk*
LinkedIn	*Sean The EQ Commando*
Facebook	*@CommandEQ* and *@EQ2Lead*
Twitter	*eq2leaduk*
Instagram	*Eq2lead*
Web	*www.eq2lead.uk*

Five Star Thinking

Joy Zarine

There are businesses across the world that rate undeniably, as five star businesses.

I don't mean that they have red carpets and butlers and present everything on silver trays. Some may have those things, but you certainly don't need to.

Five star businesses are simply exceptional. Their services or products are presented perfectly, they are unique in what they do and make the customer feel unique and special too. Five star businesses have a reputation of excellence. People who have not even experienced the business know of it and have high expectations of it when they do.

I have worked on creating five star businesses in the hospitality industry for over fifteen years. I help my clients to create incredible guest experiences that lead to five star reviews and an award winning future. But it's not only hospitality businesses that require exceptional standards and experiences.

I believe that becoming a five star business, in any industry sets you apart and offers you a far more exciting future than if you weren't one. And I want to demonstrate why you should have a five star business and exactly how you can sprinkle some five star magic into your business.

So why should you have a five star business?

Five star businesses stand out from their competition as exceptional in what they do and how they do it. For a five star restaurant for example, it means they are fully booked or have queues of people waiting in line to be served.

They have a waiting list for special events and tickets get sold out the day they are released. They have a reputation for being busy all of the time, and no one questions why, everyone knows this business is the best at what it does.

The guests who visit the business are wowed by the experience, and cannot help but tell everyone they know about it. They leave five star reviews on sites like *Tripadvisor* and *Google* because they want to tell the world how wonderful their visit was. The business impresses even when things go wrong, mistakes are swiftly rectified and the business has banked enough good grace, that the customers know it is not the norm.

It's not just the guests who are impacted by the encounter of a five star business though.

Five star businesses create a culture of passion, loyalty and exceptional standards throughout their workforce.

The employees care deeply about the work that they do and are dedicated to delivering on the mission of the business. The business rarely need to advertise for employees, because it is known as a great place to work, so they are inundated with CVs of great people keen to apply.

Outside of the business, they are making headlines for all the right reasons. The business is featured by newspapers and magazines, showcasing their events, specials, and new products and openings. No expensive adverts, they make real news showcasing all that is good and positive within the business. Five star businesses pick up awards for commitment to their community, customer service or innovations within their industry. The awards they win install a sense of pride across the team and a feeling of importance across the venue.

So what does it feel like to own a five star business?

You have a team around you who are hungry to learn from you and can cope with challenges when you are not there. You are able to go on holiday with family or friends, without fearing that the business won't be there when you return. You have a clear plan for your progress, and for the important people around you. You are a fun person to be with, both in work and out of work, never feeling stressed, never having to shout. People enjoy spending time with you, and more than that, they value your opinion. You are respected as an industry professional – one of the good ones, who is successful and passionate, knowledgeable and friendly. Your approval matters to those around you.

Five star businesses are built on strong foundations.

They don't need to discount what they sell, come up with gimmicks and constantly reinvent themselves with new names, new logos, new websites. People know who they are, and rather than just liking what they do, they love what they do, and love why they do it. And these people tell everyone they know that they love it.

So how do you ensure you build and maintain five star status within your business?

Start with the why

I am a true believer in doing work you are truly passionate about. All business owners know what their business does, some know how they do it, but not enough seem to know why.

So why do you do what you do?

Why is it so important to understand what motivates us? Well for one, when we know why we're doing something, we can be really clear about telling other people about our motivations.

When people understand why we are doing what we are doing, they can connect with us more and even believe in us more because of it. Sometimes our motivation is the only clear difference between us and all our competitors.

This means it really matters.

Often when we look at brands or businesses we love it is not because of what they do, but why they do it.

TOMS shoes are sold globally and loved by millions. They are stylish and comfortable, but in all honesty not much more than the next canvas pump. But *TOMS* have created an impact with their message of giving back. For every pair of *TOMS* shoes that is sold, a pair is donated to a person in need. Suddenly when we understand their motivation to make a positive change to the lives of others, buying a pair of canvas shoes has never felt so good.

If you can find and articulate your why, then your team, your customers and even your critics will understand what your business is really about.

Being clear about the why forms a connection with your team on a genuine human level.

Convey it in a simple message and you will change what your business stands for. Your *why* ultimately affects the how of what you do. Understanding your *why* can create the core values or purpose of your business.

Five star businesses know what matters to them and how they want to impact the world. Finding your purpose and being able to articulate it to inspire those around you sets you apart from a business owner into a business leader.

But it all starts with you asking, '*Why?*'

Connect to your customer

Too often I see businesses have lost touch with their customers. If the people at the top of the business, who make all the key decisions, disconnect with the real customers, the business may be left in a vulnerable state.

It's not enough to simply know the age range or the location of who your target market is. We need to understand who they are, how they feel, what their passions are, what are their concerns and what gets them really excited.

The most famous and successful brands do this - in what seems to be an effortless way. I assure you there is nothing effortless about it!

As business leaders we need to be able to empathise with our customers, understand what really matters to them and ensure the business aligns with their requirements.

What do our customers expect from our business, and how can we exceed those expectations? What is the experience like for a new customer? What are their frustrations, what are their concerns? How can we ensure we deliver in a better way than our competitors?

The answers to these questions are essential to understand, in order to create a five star business. Being something to everyone is impossible, but today being everything to someone is essential.

Create the exceptional

Many business have to compete not only on a local but on a global scale, so there has never been a more important time stand out as a five star business.

There are two factors to making our businesses extraordinary, *what we do* and *how we do it.*

Finding the unique product or service for your business to set you apart from the competition and help you create fame for your business can be a game-changer.

If you only ever sell the same products as everyone else in the same way as everyone else, there is nothing for anyone to get excited about. Nothing to feel passionate about.

Nothing to love. OK, there may be nothing to hate, but nothing to love? That's a very risky strategy to do business by.

If you do something remarkable, even shocking, in your business, yes, some people will hate it. But if you make your ideal customers – the key people you are targeting, get excited and love you, while all the rest hate you, then OK.

As long as there are enough people who do love you, then that's better than OK – it is exceptional. You will have a business that your people – both your team and your customers will talk about, get excited about and tell everyone about.

Deliver with consistency

One of the key factors that set five star businesses apart from everyone else is consistency. Creating an incredible buying experience once is great but if the next time you visit, it is simply not as good - then the systems aren't strong enough in your business. Meeting a customer's expectations today can be tricky, anything less than perfect for many people simply won't do. Bad reviews are bad for business so it's important to develop clear instructions and clear guidelines so you can deliver on your product or service standards every single time.

Your business will need its own set of standards to suit your style of the product or service you provide. Your standards must align with what your customer wants and expects.

You as the leader of the business will need to know them, live them, teach them and spot when something has been missed.

They have to be easy to execute every single day – no matter how quiet or busy your business is – and must be possible no matter how many team members are working. Being consistent is essential to being a five star business.

Measure success

Basking in our triumphs and victories, breaking sales records and selling out of products or events feels amazing. But when you are able to shut down any negative comments or reviews by fixing something that has been holding you and your business back, that feels pretty incredible too. Trust me!

When we investigate the facts of our customer experience and begin to measure the markers of success, we put ourselves head and shoulders above our competition. Understanding the numbers (sales, margins, spend per head, etc.) is one thing, but measuring how and what we deliver to our customer and identifying any shortcomings can be just as powerful. This requires honesty, but look at it not as a quest to find your failings, but as a fact finding mission to improve your business.

By tracking customer feedback, reviews, complaints and other measurables in your business, you can make sure you are always hitting the 1% better than yesterday mark. Because that's really all it takes. Imagine if you and your team went out to be 1% better every time you unlocked the door and switched on the lights. Imagine what your business would look like 365 days from now.

Too many businesses focus their time, energy and money on attracting new people, when if they fixed their shortcomings, their audience would never leave. It's like pouring more and more water into a bucket that is riddled with holes.

Working on your business like a pro rather than like an amateur is what sets it apart as a five star business.

For example, in the world of motor vehicles, amateur drivers bundle along on their journey, ignoring the warning signs on the dashboard, only stopping to pump up a tyre or fill up the tank when it is absolutely necessary.

The professional F1 drivers, on the other hand, surround themselves with a team of people who know their role and work on doing it quicker and better every single time.

The professional driver and their team fine-tune the engine, obsessing over improvements, practising and tweaking with every single lap.

What would happen if you approached your business in the same way, fine-tuning and improving it with every single customer?

Good service is good business

As business leaders we need to stop asking, *"How can I market my business better?"*. Because the answer to that question is never going to build you a five star business.

Five star businesses are built on the question *"How can I serve my customers better? How can I please those who come into contact with my business? How can I inspire my team to deliver on the promise of my business?"*.

These questions lead you towards becoming a five star business. Finding the answers is not easy, but when you are driven with a passion and are energised and inspired enough to want to build a better business, you will be on your way to creating one.

Many of the challenges you face in business can be overcome by focusing on not only what you do, but why you do it. Ignite passion in those around you and your business will feel more successful, more remarkable and much more like a five star business! Be sure that your customers needs and wants never stop being a focus for every single person in your business. Striving for excellence has an incredible effect on your business and everyone will notice, your team, your customers and your potential customers.

Leading a business can at times be overwhelming. When you don't know what to do for the best in your business, simply ask yourself, *"What would make this five stars?"*.

The answer to that question will always lead you in the right direction.

Joy Zarine is a hospitality and marketing consultant and the author of guest experience and hospitality book *The Five Star Formula*.

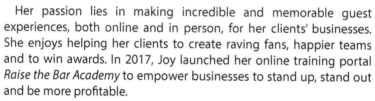

For over 15 years she has worked with industry leaders to create and market profitable and award-winning brands.

From humble bartending beginnings in her teens, Joy has gone on to help launch UK-wide brands and create her own marketing consultancy to support hospitality businesses, especially cocktail bars, gastro pubs and restaurants.

Her passion lies in making incredible and memorable guest experiences, both online and in person, for her clients' businesses. She enjoys helping her clients to create raving fans, happier teams and to win awards. In 2017, Joy launched her online training portal *Raise the Bar Academy* to empower businesses to stand up, stand out and be more profitable.

The *Five Star Formula* is Joy's first book; she is currently writing her second book, *The Voice of Experience,* which is scheduled to be released in Autumn 2018.

Twitter	*@JoyZarine*
Facebook	*Facebook.com/joyzarineltd*
Web	*www.joyzarine.com*

The Future Belongs To Those Who Can Focus

Dan Browne

We are well on our way into the *information age*. Technology is ushering a new era of ever increasing productivity – we have the ability to produce a lot more than we could do even five years ago. This has great advantages for business, education and progress in general but it is not without its pitfalls.

Namely distraction, overwhelm and overworking.

Having worked in many different companies as a strategy consultant, I've noticed an increase in the number of hours that many leaders work. In fact a study of attitudes to work by the *Smith Institute*, in 2016, found that two thirds of people were spending more time at work with little gains in productivity, and more than a quarter of staff believed their productivity had declined over the past two years.

People are feeling frazzled and stressed out.

Coupled with increasing workloads are the demand on our attention, from smart phones and social media to stalking and intrusive advertising. Our attention is being diverted.

Apps and games are designed to stimulate us to engage with them. Click bait articles use psychology to prompt us to click on them. There is a war for our attention.

While we are trying to be productive by working longer, our attention is being solicited by *Apps* and ads designed to distract.

This scattered focus is draining on our mental energy reserves. Our brains are hyper active or in a state of hypervigilance. Information overload!

As leaders, this is our new playing field. There is a call for us to have higher levels of clarity and focus to be able to rise above the noise and navigate to where we need to go. We also need to help our teams and communities who are also at risk of distraction.

As the workforce gets younger, with people who have grown into a world of technology and never known life without smartphones, we need to be able to deal with others who may have never lived in less distracting times.

In my experience *Millennials,* while they are brilliant in their facility with technology their ability to focus can sometimes be a problem.

Our instinctive approach to the information overload is fight or flight.

When we get overwhelmed by what we have to do, we will go into one of two modes: *fight* or *flight*. This is instinctual.

Fight approach

The *fight* aspect is how most driven people react. We go to conquer the work. We put more hours in we over schedule, we multi task. However, this approach limits our productivity.

A study by the university of California following American information workers found that time spent focusing on one task at a time was 59.5 seconds. Meaning workers were shifting their focus every minute. This had reduced from three minutes in 2012. So, a significant increase in multi-tasking.

A second study showed that the average office worker is distracted every 11 mins and once distracted it takes them 25 minutes to refocus on their task. You can imagine with this level of distraction we are getting less done that we could and end up either working longer to compensate or we have the background worry of how much work we have to get done.

Denial approach
The other approach is *flight* or *denial*. Keeping away from interruption to get stuff done. While this is a good temporary measure for a day it is not an effective long-term strategy.

I found this a problem at a client company, employees had a culture of making themselves *uninterruptible* to the point that it was difficult to get things done. People would avoid interaction because they were overwhelmed.

They would work from home, work away from their desks, avoid answering emails, anything to avoid being interrupted. Effectively hiding.

The impact on the team however was that an inordinate amount of time was spent tracking employees at a cost of other people's time. So, denial while it may seem convenient for the person shutting everyone out, has an impact on the rest of the team and doesn't earn you a reputation of being a team player.

The greater impact on ourselves
Beyond the workplace the impact on distraction is on our personal lives. When you are with loved ones and friends, your thoughts are concerned with of all the things that you should have done and you don't bring the level of focus to the people that you are with.

I'm sure you've been on the receiving end of someone not listening or pretending to listen. At first innocuous, over time it breeds resentment with people impacting relationships, friendships and marriages. One party doesn't feel listened to then withholds their listening and attention, even sometimes turning to someone or something else for attention.

What is needed is the balance. The need to strike the balance between the usefulness of our tech without getting distracted by it.

Distraction is habit forming

According to neuroscience distraction can be habit forming. The brain likes to form habitual ways of thinking, feeling and acting. This is *neuroplasticity,* the brain conserves energy by hard wiring repeated behaviours (skills) and thinking patterns (personality) so that who we are, our thoughts and behaviours become automatic habits. Whenever we learn something new, it requires a lot of learning and brain power as our brain forms new neural connections for that skill or habit. But over time as these learnings are entrained this is what we become. If you get used to being distracted, the brain adapts itself for this state and it becomes the norm, focusing becomes difficult.

Conversely focus can be built like building a muscle.

Introducing the brain

There are three regions of the brain that impact our thinking process.

The *amygdala* or the *reptilian brain.* This the instinctual part of the brain that deals with *survival;* fight or flight. When stressed we are in the throes of the amygdala alert to danger everywhere.

Limbic or *mammalian brain* this is our *emotional* centre. When this part is in control we want familiarity, comfort and pleasure, this includes habits and addictions.

The *frontal cortex* – is the higher seat of our *thinking.*

When we are creative, logical and /or focused we are using this part of the brain.

When we find ourselves stressed or engaged in habitual or distracting behaviour we need to be aware that we are not in our best state for thinking. A handy trick when stressed is to put your attention in the space behind your forehead and just notice what you feel. Putting your attention there stimulates the frontal cortex.

Amygdala	Limbic	Frontal Cortex
Reptilian Brain	Mammalian Brain	Human Brain
Instinct Flight/Fight	Emotions and habits	Logic,Thinking, Creativity

The power of focus

Humans have shown great ability to focus. Monks meditating in the Himalayas can increase their body temperature by focus and an intense level of concentration. For us mere mortals who don't spend a lot of time meditating, the benefit of being able to focus enables us to get into flow and do our best work, have more willpower and be better listeners.

How to develop focus

Focus like a muscle it is something that can be strengthened. We train the neural pathways in our brain to let go of distraction and to focus.

Here are some great exercises to help us free ourselves from distraction.

Sit with distraction

We are always trying to get away from ourselves.

The ability to sit with ourselves when it is uncomfortable, when you want to be distracted is essential. If we react to the impulse for distraction we are feeding these distraction circuits in the brain. When we can sit with distraction we are tuning out the noise and strengthening our ability to concentrate.

Limit your news intake

Most news is all about fear. News stimulates the reptilian and mammalian part of our brain the part that is all about survival. This is the reason why we tune in to the news and why the news functions the way it does. Studies show that we have a bias for negative news.

Unless your job specifically requires it, limit your news to what's necessary and avoid it first thing in the morning. Make it a conscious act rather than an automatic reaction. Trial it.

Take a week with a news diet and see how you feel vs. being constantly bombarded by news.

Give your brain a rest

Our brains are designed to help us figure life out but often we will ruminate on subjects that are unsolvable or not worth our time. Our brains aren't supposed to work all day like any organ it needs stimulus and rest. Take time off to not think, to have no brain activity. That includes giving up worrying and ruminating.

Take a tech sabbath

I got this practice from a friend of mine: Orthodox Jews on the sabbath avoid using technology from the beginning of the sabbath o Friday sundown to Saturday sun down. Weekly or twice weekly take a tech sabbath avoid using any data driven technology.

Do not use your computer, tablet or smartphone (only use it as a phone). I found this invaluable, I would notice my unconscious tendency to reach for my phone. Over time I got a greater sense of peace, relaxation and peace of mind.

Meditation

Can be passive as well as active. The passive version known as mindfulness is sitting and noticing your thoughts and feelings. This is perfect for getting out of the distraction habit. Active meditation helps to increase focus.

For more info on meditation visit my website at *www.danielebrowne.com* or read my book *The Energy Equation – how to be a top performer without burning yourself out.*

Read complicated books that require you to focus and develop concentration

An expression of the millennial generation is TL: DR (*too long didn't read)* – the avoidance of long texts.

Unfortunately avoiding complication makes us intellectually lazy and thinking becomes more effortful. Take time to read long texts that you are interested in.

This encourages the development of focus.

Using structure for your life and teams

The best way to entrain new habits is to create habits to enforce them. I like to talk about structure. Structure is a collection of systems and practices used to entrain habits and achieve results. Structure works for you as an individual or a team.

In my book, the energy equation I talk about structure for productivity.

There are four elements of structure:

- **Agreements** – what you agree to your stated goals and intentions as well a formal verbal or written agreements
- **People** – the people who are involved or support you in your endeavour
- **Environment** – the physical environment where you do your work
- **Time** when you choose to do your work.

The four factors essentially answer the question *What, With Whom, Where* and *When*. And you can create as structure for anything. For better relationships, increased fitness, better work performance. Structure in teams is very useful. Below are some examples of best practices.

Agreements

Agreements and written goals provide clarity. What are your stated goals and intentions? What will you take on doing or not doing? Write these down. Manage these agreements so that you are aware of them regularly, use project management software, a whiteboard or *Apps* such as *Asana* or *Trello*.

People

The teams and support people you work with can enhance or hinder your progress. High performers work in teams or have support staff, they have the right people in the right roles. They use coaches and /or accountability groups. The key to making teams work is regular accountability and project updates.

Environment

The environment is critical for performance we need different environments for different tasks. When I'm writing I usually like a quiet place such as home or a coffee shop but I like a busy office and colleagues to interact with when I'm not writing.

One of my clients a large corporate has a large open plan office with multiple zones for productivity. They have high tables and bar stools for collaboration, private booths for individual focused work, telephone booths for phone conversations, stand up meeting rooms for quick pow wows and quiet zones. The ability to move to different zones greatly facilitates the different types of work people do and their preferences.

Time

Timetable when you'll do the work and how much time you allocate.

Scheduling your timetable for your own personal work style and your team is an art and science. Some people are more effective in the morning some in the evening. Creating a schedule that works for the team is powerful. In my early days, I worked in a firm that taught high performance courses. One of the key practices we took on was having blocks of uninterrupted times. You could only interrupt people for 15 minutes every two hours. So, everyone could work undistracted for two hours. There was an exception if you needed someone urgently. Other than that, you would a schedule meeting if you needed to work with someone. This was a highly effective process.

These practices seem simple but when you sit down and design an environment for focus and performance you'll see performance sky rocket. See what best practices you can incorporate in your structure.

The future belongs to those who focus as we live in a world that is constantly distracting us and training us to be recipients of news, information and advertising. We will lose some of our ability to focus if we don't take back control of our minds.

As leaders, this is our responsibility.

Daniel Browne is an expert in productivity, performance and wellbeing, Daniel specialises in helping leaders and teams get better results by elevating their improving their energy and effectiveness while keeping a work life balance

Daniel started his career working in an investment bank in the city and has worked in extremely demanding jobs ever since in finance and strategy consulting.

After a few years, working over 12 hours a day (often working through the night, sacrificing weekends and a social life) started to take its toll.

Daniel was exhausted and really concerned about his wellbeing. There had to be a more efficient way to perform well at work and still have a life.

Daniel started researching alternative methods of performance improvement. He studied everything from mediation, yoga, Tai Chi, neuroscience, relaxation techniques and even hypnotherapy. He then created a program designed to meet the needs of people working in demanding jobs with little time to spare for anything else.

This was work culminated in the book, *The Energy Equation: How to be a top performer without burning yourself out*, which became a best seller in the *WHSmith* business book charts.

Social

Quality of life, quality of experience,
quality of environment, connection to family,
friends, community, work, social,
relationships, stress

Impostor in Your Team

Tara Halliday

People are the key to your business success, and none more so than your executive team. When your team is working at their greatest potential, it feels like there's nothing you can't achieve. As their leader, you look for areas to improve and try to spot issues before they become a big problem.

But there is a destructive issue that affects 70% of high-achievers at some point in their lives. It creates stress-related illness, addictions, volatile behaviour, burnout and people simply quitting. And by its very nature, it is kept a complete secret.

I'm talking here about *Impostor Syndrome*. The *Impostor Syndrome* is not a medically-defined mental health syndrome, but it is a *phenomenon*; an observed pattern of behaviour.

It's the secret feeling of being a fraud and the fear of being *found out*. At first it can seem absurd; your carefully selected team are bright, capable, confident, talented and committed. That such successful people might feel like they're *a fraud* or *not good enough* – appears counterintuitive.

Yet certain situations can trigger a latent belief that society teaches everyone from a young age; that our worth depends on what we do.

It's a belief so prevalent we don't even notice it and rarely question it. Indeed the drive to prove our worth is often at the heart of an ambitious personality.

This latent belief turns into *Impostor Syndrome* when it taps into a specific event or role which is especially important to that person. They have attached their worth to doing well and not failing in that one thing. That event or role depends on the individual, so you can't predict it in advance. And it's unlikely your team could predict it either.

Even so, once it has struck then your team member develops an anxiety that they are not good enough. They think that they're fooling everyone – especially you. That you must have made a mistake in hiring them, or it was pure luck, or they had some unfair help.

They become *hypervigilant* that someone will find out that they're not as good as you think they are.

As the anxiety increases their hard work becomes overwork, putting far more time and effort into a project than it needs. They also become *perfectionistic*, intolerant of any mistakes and will take to hiding mistakes.

Their independence turns into a refusal to ask for help, as they fear it will expose their *weaknesses*. The stress may cause them to develop volatile behaviours. Relationships at work and home may suffer, and they may turn to addictive behaviours to try and cope with the anxiety.

Above all, they're going to try and hold it together, act as if nothing is wrong and not discuss it with their colleagues and certainly not you, their boss.

Often a leader does not know about the problem until the crisis hits. Either the team member leaves due to burnout, a hidden mistake becomes a critical issue, or they quit with no real explanation.

What can you do?

So what can you do to help your team members if or when they suffer from *Impostor Syndrome*? How can you protect your business from such a management team crisis?

What you *can't* do is try to spot it, vet your team for it and avoid hiring anyone who might be *at risk* from *Impostor Syndrome*. This is because everyone is operating under the same latent core belief that our worth depends on what we do. It can affect anyone.

Nor is it a flaw or silly childish thinking that we ought to grow out of. It is a fundamental belief about the way we operate and survive in the world. It is as significant and constant as gravity. And as invisible.

There's no point asking your team about it either. If they are feeling like an impostor, they would be unlikely to reveal that fact to you. Also, they are unlikely to understand what's going on themselves. Unless they are aware of *Impostor Syndrome*, its prevalence and its common symptoms, then your team member will be confused.

They will be struck by a feeling of not being good enough when they're used to feeling confident and capable. They will develop anxiety and not know the cause. They will feel isolated, thinking it must be just them. They will compare themselves to you and their colleagues, and to your confidence and success. They develop a growing sense that they don't belong on the team. They worry that somehow they have become flawed and weak. And they fear that at any time you're going to realise they don't belong and fire them.

The exact circumstances that set off *Impostor Syndrome* are unique to the individual. But, there are two major triggers to *Impostor Syndrome*. This means that you can create conditions in which *Impostor Syndrome* is less likely to become a problem. You can mitigate the effects on your team and your business.

Trigger 1: Change

When someone moves out of their comfort zone, there is a risk of triggering *Impostor Syndrome*. Especially in a new role or doing something outside of their realm of expertise. Sufferers of *Impostor Syndrome* often avoid situations in which they might feel not good enough.

For example, I was uncomfortable with one small aspect of team management. After University, my psychological profile test results prompted a company to offer me a fast-track to top management. At the time I was completely unaware of my motivation, but I turned down this fabulous offer. Instead I went back to University. I have a PhD because my *Impostor Syndrome* fears of team management had me avoid that situation.

When I became a Director in a high-tech startup, I had a larger team to manage. Then the stress of *Impostor Syndrome* hit me. I didn't see it as being a fraud in the classic sense, I felt like my *failure* to excel was a fundamental flaw in who I am. This is not uncommon.

This example shows that anytime someone steps into new territory, it may trigger Impostor Syndrome as they may have been avoiding it. If this new territory happens to include their individual 'worth trigger', then their stress will increase, and their performance will suffer. You cannot predict who might get triggered or in what circumstances, but you can put in place some procedures that will help.

Strategies for Change

There are some simple strategies that you can implement that are effective at helping your team through change. These apply to everyone equally so that people don't feel singled out. They make good business sense as well as proactively mitigating *Impostor Syndrome*.

- Provide training
- Plan for assistance
- Provide transition support

Provide Training

In new territory, there will be some areas with which your team are unfamiliar. But they may be reluctant to ask for extra skills training, for fear of looking weak or incompetent to you. They may feel a need to prove themselves (their worth) to you by going it alone or figuring it out for themselves.

Instead, you can require them to take some training to upgrade their skills because it is a new role or project, or change. Set up in this way, the training is not seen as a weakness or flaw in your team member. Instead, it is your proactive strategy for excellence. This makes sure the project or role is as successful as possible in every way. It is also good practice for continual professional development.

In the example of my *Impostor Syndrome,* the issue was a lack of skill in certain team dynamics. Looking into my past I see I never had good team management modelled; my family did not know how, not their fault. My boss at the start-up company was a brilliant team manager. He would have been delighted to mentor me, had I only asked. I didn't see the issue to be my lack of skill, and so it never occurred to me to ask.

To mitigate *Impostor Syndrome*, the training you offer needs to be the right skill. Here simply discuss the areas in the new role/project with which the team member is most and least comfortable. The training will then be in the areas of discomfort.

Plan for Assistance

Many people suffering from *Impostor Syndrome* are reluctant to ask for help in any form, even when they need it.

They view asking for help as an admission of weakness, and it will reveal they are a fraud and not good enough.

You can't force people to ask for help. But you can ask them who they will be getting to help them and whether their project or role has enough resources to be successful. You make the explicit statement that assistance will be required to make this successful. This is a strategy for excellence and not a criticism of their worth or capability.

When you ask this in a team meeting, it models planning the resources for success to the whole team. It normalises asking for assistance to get the best results. Anyone who tries to look *tough* and do it by themselves can be reminded that success is a team effort.

A classic source of anxiety in *Impostor Syndrome* comes from comparing themselves to colleagues. It is important for sufferers to be able to see their colleagues asking for help.

This needs to balance within your company structure, of course. If people resources are tight, then your team has some negotiation to do. Watch out for someone who tries to make a virtue of pushing through with superhuman effort. This can backfire, becoming a trigger for *Impostor Syndrome* in the rest of the team, or in themselves.

Provide Transition Support

With any major change in role, responsibilities and projects, several issues will arise for that team member. It may be *Impostor Syndrome* or it may be that adjustments need to be made and new relationships navigated.

One of the best ways to help *Impostor Syndrome* is for sufferers to share their situation and fears with a neutral party. A great strategy is to offer transition coaching outside the company with a professional who is not reporting back to you. It is a service offered to your team member for their support.

If you are tempted to bring this in-house then you should be aware that with *Impostor Syndrome*, anyone at work finding out is a disaster, and so it is unlikely to be helpful.

Trigger 2: Negative Environment

Impostor Syndrome has its roots in learning that our worth depends on what we do. That is, if a child is obedient, quiet, does well in school, then they are likely to get approval. But if they are noisy, disobedient, messy, make mistakes, then the attitude of adults changes around them. The child sees frowns, sighs or more obvious anger. Regardless of the subtlety of the delivery, the message is clear. Children conclude that when they don't get things right, then they are bad. Not worthwhile.

This is not taught deliberately in our society, so there is no blame for any adults here. We teach our children the world as we know it.

What it means for your team is that a negative or critical environment can also become a trigger for *Impostor Syndrome* in adults. It can be helpful to review the tone of your interaction with your team and between your team.

As a leader you will take on a defacto *parent* position for your team, as anyone with authority does. It is normal psychological behaviour in humans.

This means that your actions, in particular, can help reduce the effect of *Impostor Syndrome* in several areas.

- Making mistakes
- Tone of meeting
- Positive regard

Making Mistakes

Intolerance of making mistakes is a hallmark of *Impostor Syndrome*. The assumption is that if I make a mistake (in the one area on which my worth depends) then I am bad/flawed/worthless and a fraud. But it is an unconscious assumption.

Generally *Impostor Syndrome* sufferers experience a vague anxiety, or beat themselves up when they make mistakes.

The solution appears to be perfectionism, overwork and hiding mistakes. The real solution is to work in an environment where mistakes are acceptable and used to learn personally and as a business.

Acceptance of mistakes means not being angry, disappointed or blaming when a mistake is revealed. Seeing it as an opportunity to teach or to refine the business systems is very helpful.

Accepting mistakes does not mean condoning low standards, though. Every mistake should have a learning come out of it, so that it is not repeated, or new checks put in place to catch it before it becomes a problem. This kind of positive teaching and learning environment makes the team more comfortable. It gives them more access to their creativity when looking for solutions too.

Tone of Meeting

The tone of any meeting should reflect the acceptance of ideas and opinions without ridicule or humiliation. Most of the time your team members will be resilient to banter, however when it turns into anger and sniping then it becomes destructive.

This is where a leader needs to have great self-awareness and commitment. It's not easy to challenge our own behaviour as a possible source of the problem. The tone of a meeting is set by you, and you create the rules for conduct within the meeting.

Positive regard

Certain positive behaviours from a leader are a tremendous help against *Impostor* feelings. But they have to be the right ones to actually help.

Praising people for success does not actually help when they feel like an Impostor. In fact it makes them feel more isolated and unseen. A better approach is to ask what they enjoyed about their success/project, and what did they learn from it. This helps them claim the success as their own.

Another powerful behaviour is to give your team members your undivided attention when they are talking to you. Multitasking someone makes them feel unimportant to you. When you stop reading, checking emails or texts when they are speaking, you convey a strong message that they are important to you and that they belong there. That they are, indeed, good enough.

Impostor Syndrome is more common in successful people than anyone likes to admit. It is not a weakness or flaw, however. Certain procedures and attitudes that promote excellence also help eliminate *Impostor Syndrome*.

These few changes will positively impact your whole team. You cannot predict who will develop *Impostor Syndrome,* or when. Yet your proactive choices make it much less likely to develop and turn into a crisis.

Prevention is a much easier path.

Tara Halliday helps successful executives and professionals reach even greater heights through a unique blend of coaching, therapy and teaching.

She restructures *Mindset, Heartset* and *Core Beliefs* to clear away deep-seated blocks to peak performance.

Tara has a PhD in Engineering and 16 years as a therapist and coach. She provides 6-month, intensive one-to-one development programmes that leave you feeling calm, fearless and invincible. This programme includes overcoming *Impostor Syndrome,* where necessary.

Tara delivers an online self-help course for *Impostor Syndrome* sufferers, as well as three-day retreats for their deeper healing. She is also the author of *The Coach's Guide to Impostor Syndrome.*

Web   *www.completesuccess.co.uk*

Email   *tara@completesuccess.co.uk*

Maintaining Family and Work Life Balance in an Ever Changing Worlds

Robert James

We live in a time of the most rapid change the world has ever experienced. It feels like everything is changing constantly.

Families are under many pressures; both externally and internally. Have you ever felt like your world is charging so quickly that you just can't keep up with it? At times, it probably feels like you are constantly chasing a moving target; and it's totally unreachable. Like a greyhound chasing a mechanical rabbit that just keeps going faster.

We are now connected to the virtual world 24/7. The family life is not as clearly separated from the business world as it used to be. Social media has changed the way we build relationships and how we spend our family time.

Let's add another layer to this. The reality is that your own personal world is changing as well. Over the next few years, things will change in your family life. You may get married, you may get divorced. Maybe your family will grow—perhaps you will have your first child, or your fourth; or your first-born may leave home.

It's even possible that you could lose your current job or start a new business. You may become a millionaire or you might even go bankrupt. Maybe your parents will pass or you lose a child. How about you finally write that book you've always been planning to write? You may just take up yoga or decide to eat healthier and lose weight. On top of all of this, there are the things that other people do or don't that you cannot control, that can certainly put your world in a spin. All these factors impact the daily balance in your family and work life.

As humans, we have a true desire to have meaningful relationships with other humans; we are a herd animal by nature. Solitary confinement is the worst punishment you can do to a human. So, when we are out of balance with the key relationships in our lives, it rocks us on many levels.

The real secret to this is having a handle on your own personal ethics. Those things that are really, truly important to you in the long run. Then always act within your personal ethics. This is not about what others expect of you, but about what you expect of yourself.

Each day you will be faced with choices on where you put your energy. Most of these are small, every day decisions that determine your direction over every aspect of your life, progressively heading towards your long-term outcome. You decide these decisions, they are within your control.

Martha

The toughest challenges will come when the outside world hits you from left field with the *knock out* punch that you never could have seen coming. How will you react when your world gets turned upside down?

Martha is an excellent example of how to actively recalibrate the family/work balance in a constantly moving world. Martha was born and raised in South Africa; and grew up during a time of rapid change in her homeland. She was raised primarily by her mother—a teacher with a passion for science who also did quite a bit of charity work for her local community.

Martha describes her mum as, "The most amazing, strong, loving woman I have ever known." For the most part, her father was *absent* while she was growing up. Something she doesn't really feel impacted her all that much.

"My mother was such a strong woman that I never even noticed he wasn't around until I was much older, and you can't miss what you don't know" she recently told me.

Life was very good for Martha and her mother, despite the political unrest. Martha got her degree in engineering, and met a wonderful man while she was at University who also became an engineer. After school, they both started their careers and then got married. A little later, along came their son and daughter. Her own world had changed for the better but South Africa was becoming a very unstable environment to live in.

One day, that political unrest changed everything. Martha's mother had worked for many years in a soup kitchen for the homeless. On this fateful day, a man from the soup kitchen followed her home, broke into her house, and took her life. A stranger who her mother had helped just hours earlier, senselessly murdered this caring woman. Martha's world was turned completely upside down.

As the months passed, it become clear to Martha and her husband that their future was not in South Africa. It was time to find a home to give her children a safer future. They applied to emigrate to Australia and were accepted. They packed up their young family and headed to the other side of the world; a brave new start leaving their heartache behind them.

Major events can instigate major changes for all of us. These changes are happening to people all around us every day. How you react to the changes will decide if you can regain your balance.

The engineering careers of Martha and her husband were the key asset that gave them the opportunity to emigrate to Australia. The opportunity to rebuild in Australia was on the back of their skills and work history. Not long after arriving they both got new jobs. Then Martha's career took off and she really found her place in Australia.

Unfortunately, her husband did not settle into the new life as comfortably. His first engineering job didn't even last six months. He struggled and couldn't find full-time work in his field. He was the children's primary caregiver while he searched for his new direction.

As the years passed, their balance never really recovered. Martha was carrying the financial load for the entire family. Now in a senior leadership role in her field, she had a good income and they could live comfortably.

The impact of the change however, became a major struggle for her husband. He tried various career paths, but nothing really worked out for him. His mental health was suffering, his behaviour difficult, aggressive and irrational. Their own home has now become the *volatile* environment that they left behind in South Africa.

Martha found herself working later and later, and even finding work-related excuses to avoid being at home. Work became her escape from the harsh reality of what her home life had become. It was much easier to be working than to be dealing with a husband whose mental health was deteriorating more and more each day.

Her husband had become emotionally and verbally abusive. When she did arrive home, he resented her working. He would go out and not come home until the early the next morning. One morning, she found the car in the driveway with damage all down one side and he couldn't even recall how it got there.

Martha was missing time with her children to avoid time with her husband. She came to the realization that the marriage had become completely dysfunctional. For the good of the whole family, it was time to finish the marriage. "The day I told him was very tough. I must admit I have a problem dealing with conflict" she said. "I knew I had to do it, when I did he fell to the floor grabbed my leg and begged me not to go. But, I had to get my freedom."

The principal goals for Martha had always been to supply a safe environment for her children to grow up in and to have a rewarding career. They left their homeland and found Australia to be a safe place, full of opportunities. Her career had reached heights not possible in South Africa. Her children were now 14 and 12 and both were doing well in a good school.

Martha adapted to the changes, and with each step she rebalanced and stayed focused on the long-term outcome. In the turmoil of everyday drama, it can be very easy to rationalize a way to not have to deal with an issue, such as ending a long-term relationship.

She could not control the actions and responses of her husband.

She often bought into his rationalisations and stayed comfortable by not confronting him regarding his unacceptable behaviour. Her husband struggled with each and every step of the changes; pressure changes some people for the better, others not so much. "He was not the man I married, he changed!"

It takes pragmatism to deal with these high-level changes. Many people struggle and everyone is affected to varying degrees. It also takes pragmatism to mend the bridges and to move forward. Once the heat of the separation was done, her family found a newer, much more comfortable balance. The children are living in a shared parenting arrangement. Her ex-husband has found a new partner, and Martha even attended the wedding and shared a dance with him.

The violent death of her mother triggered the journey to a new country. The changes presented great opportunities but also created instability in their home.

Martha had to actively deal with the change. Her ability to stay clear on the long-term outcome got her there. When she avoided dealing with the unacceptable behaviour of her husband, the problems at home just got more out of control. The balance of her family went into a spin.

In the short term, it can be easier to emigrate to a new country than it is to deal with the unacceptable behaviour of someone close to you. Our own comfort zones can be the biggest blocks when it comes to a true family/work-life balance. You have to get uncomfortable to deal with issues that have an emotional charge to move forward. Sometimes, it can be easier to work longer hours than it is to go home and deal with a family member.

The keys to maintaining a family/work-life balance in this forever moving world:

Find Your Own True North

When you get a good handle on what is important to you, it gives you clarity in your decision-making process; with the big decisions and the little, daily ones. Like a compass on a ship at sea, even when you can't see the shore, it will guide you to keep you on your course. Take the time to get this clear in your mind and that of your life partner. Hopefully, you share the same *True North*. If not, it's probably time to sit down and talk about it.

Take Responsibility to Actively Stay on Course

The key relationships in our life are the areas that have the most impact on you. Evaluate whether or not you are investing the right ratio of your time. This is an ever-changing ratio.

Remember, your parents still need you and you still need them. As they age the roles will reverse, if you are fortunate enough to have parents live into old age. You will find them in the position to need you in a different way.

If you have a VIP life partner, then invest daily in communicating to keep you both heading on the same course. Without open, honest communication you won't both stay on the same course.

Key relationships include the people in your work environment. These are commercial relationships and understand that no matter how great the relationships are with work colleagues, it is still based on a *financial arrangement*. Employees will take the better job offer or your boss could lay you off next month, without giving it a second thought.

If something in your life is out of balance, take action today. Sometimes it is huge action like emigrating to Australia or just telling your partner what you are really thinking and feeling. Maybe not staying the extra hour at work.

Not Carrying the Past Forward

When the *Emotional Storm* hits, the danger is learning the wrong lesson. Stuff happens to all families. It is not fair; the world is not fair. Bad things happen to good people all the time. For some, it becomes a weight they carry forward. The weight of the sadness can be a lifelong burden, or it can be a lesson to appreciate the moment and the people around you.

People in your life are going to do the w*rong thing* by you. People close to you may *break your heart*. A stranger may take someone or something of great value away from you. It may be wrong and totally unjustified.

A stranger violently took Martha's mother from her. I asked how she moved on from such a heart-breaking loss at the hands of a stranger. She said, "I have found that forgiving people makes it so much easier to move on. When you *hold on* to a grudge, no matter how justified, you are effectively holding on to a person too. I prefer to live my life free of the people and circumstances that cause me grief, and to be happy in each and every moment. It sounds a bit cheesy written down like that, but that is my philosophy and it seems to have worked OK so far." Martha's are words to live by—accept what happened and move on.

Quickly Adapting to the Changes

When the *weather* changes, you do need to re-calibrate and re-adjust. We can get caught up in the external changes in our world. Our world is changing on all levels.

Social media changes the way we perceive this world as well; people living their lives in a virtual world. Having the most *Likes* and how many *Facebook* friends you have seem to be distracting us all from the real world.

We now even see tribute pages for people who have passed away. I do often wonder if in ten years will we be doing *Facebook Live* at our funerals. Are we going to value people's lives by how many followers, likes, comments, or shares they had? The real key, I think, is to quickly adapt to the changes while managing to stay true to your own direction.

Hanging in There and Staying Focused on the Long-term

The race is long and in the end, it is only with yourself. The challenge of *getting it right* when balancing the family and business life struggle is a work in progress. If you keep working on it then you will progress. When you get it right, you will be living the life you've always dreamed of.

At *Balance Enterprises*, our goal is to empower business owners to get their businesses to work for their families. We believe if the balance is right the business will fly. Nothing is more rewarding than getting it right.

Robert James has a proven record in business. He is passionate about growing business while maintaining his connection with his family. At the age of 21 he first entered the business world as a professional horse trainer and breaker. By 27 years of age he had commenced his franchise network *James Home Service,* which grew to a 400-strong franchise  system and turned over $20 million in home services annually. And he has over 20 years of experience as an elite business coach and sales manager.

Robert is also a devoted dad to five cool kids Hayden, Cameron, Nadine, Rohan and Luke. He has been there main caregiver for nearly 20 years. Robert truly lives and breathes that "Your business should work for your family."

Robert is the author of *"Balance: How to make your family and business life work together.* Where he shares his experiences to show how you can have both a great business and a strong family life.

The latest James' family business is *Balance Enterprises,* empowering family business owners to take control, to give them the family the business life balance they require for long term success.

If you are struggling and are looking to get the direction right, read *Balance—How to make your business and family life work together.*

Web   *https://balance.enterprise*

Meaning and Purpose

**Spiritual, values, ethics,
moral behaviours, legacy, generativity,
rehearsing the future**

The Dao of Leadership

Ben Green

Let's start by pronouncing the word correctly.

Dao rhymes with *cow* and as with many of the Chinese characters, it has multiple meanings. A common translation of the word *Dao* is that it means *Path*.

This suggests that leadership (and life) is a journey and as such is something that we must experience and respond to from moment to moment. We don't know for sure what is around the next corner but we can familiarise ourselves with certain principles that will give us options and provide a guiding light for dealing with any eventuality.

People who learn about the principles of the *Dao* are called Daoists and the body of wisdom that they learn about is called Daoism. It has been around for tens of thousands of years and has influenced leaders at every level throughout time. The Daoists were basically the first life coaches on the planet and they compiled guidelines for every aspect of living a successful harmonious life.

Daoism is considered a science, a culture, a philosophy and a religion. You can learn about, practice and benefit from its wisdom without ever having to set foot in a temple or adopt any of its religious aspects. Although it has its roots in China, the senior Daoists that I have met say that it is a gift for the world for people of every nation, race and ethnicity to benefit from.

The principles were deduced from observing the flows of energy in nature and in human interactions. In business or in any leadership role, it is important to have your finger on the pulse of the organisation and the wider environment to help guide employees, steer activities and avoid mishaps. It is for this reason that the emperors of old and the politicians of modern China consult with Daoists and pay heed to their counsel on matters of governance.

Understanding the different characters who you meet and work with is a key skill of any leader. Being able to sense a person's strengths and how they might behave in different circumstances, makes a huge difference in your ability to get results from your team.

Having an awareness of the bigger picture, of the effects of decisions and actions and having an ability to factor these longer-range consequences is crucial to being effective in a leadership role.

Yin and Yang

From a Daoist perspective, the starting point for unpicking and observing patterns that can help guide our actions is to learn about the two fundamental energies of yin and yang. By gaining an appreciation of their differences and how they interact we are better placed to read people, events and opportunities.

We can then harmonise with them to get the best results.

To understand the meaning of yin and yang it is useful to imagine a hill. One side of the hill is south facing and receives a great deal of sun through the day. The other side is north facing and is always in the shade.

If you were to take a walk on the sunny side you might notice lush vegetation bursting outwards with colour and leaves and flowers. There might be many insects that have come to feast on the vibrant plant-life and in turn many birds that are here for the insects and the berries. As you walk you might notice how hard you are working to push your way upwards and you might stop to cast your eyes far and wide whilst taking a deep breath and expanding your chest. You probably feel yourself getting hot and want to cast off clothes as your body pushes moisture and heat out in an effort to cool down.

Once you reach the summit and feel the sun beating down on you it will come as a welcome change as you feel the pull of gravity and descend into the cooler, shadier side of the hill. You notice that it is darker and the vegetation is darker too. There is less activity and consequently it feels more peaceful.

Rather than looking outwards at the view, your focus narrows as you watch your step and maybe turn inwards to be more reflective. The longer you walk through the shade the cooler your body becomes and you will start to pull clothes around you to keep your heat in. Your body language closes as your muscles tighten, shoulders round and pull your blood inwards to your organs.

Yin and yang are sometimes presented as opposites but it is also important to understand them as complimentary. When the sun is too yang, the cool yin of the shade brings balance. When the cool shade is too much then the yang heat of the sun brings much needed warmth and energy.

Everything exists on a scale from yin to yang. Even at the extreme ends of the scale, the seeds of the opposite are contained. At the most yang point of summer, the transition to a yin phase has already begun. When we reach the depths of winter, the gradual return of spring is already in motion.

So, how does this relate to leadership?

There are times when a yang approach is the correct course of action. Expressing your views with energy. Setting clear deadlines and holding people to account. Driving people forwards and pushing for massive action are all necessary and valuable ways of being. However, just as we seek the shelter of the shade after extended periods in the sun, a team exposed to an unrelenting yang approach will seek ways to balance the environment. This might take the form of more yin behaviour and activities.

Maybe they will take *duvet days* to find the rest and calm they need. Perhaps they will withdraw inwards and be less forth coming, or just offer the answers you want to hear but behind those responses, there is emptiness. Things they say will be done, don't get done.

Perhaps, through fear of the consequences, they will hold information back from you and not share their real thoughts and feelings. At the most extreme, a persistent yang approach can lead to over-exertion, tiredness, depleted energy, illness, days off work and ultimately the final withdrawal of leaving the organisation.

To counteract the yin effects of an overly yang approach, the best leaders are able to sense when it is time to be more yin. A little cooler, maybe more hands-off, trusting their team to explore and make their own mistakes, maybe even encouraging it. Instead of telling and directing proceedings, asking employees for their thoughts and listening to what their challenges are. This might involve expressing yourself in a more caring nurturing way and showing concern for team-members well-being.

To counteract the yang activity of work, maybe you can think of ways to provide opportunities for rest and social time and enjoying being in the company of colleagues as fellow humans rather than fellow workers.

In the same way that it is important to balance the books

and ensure the finances of an organisation are sustainable, it is equally important to balance the energy of a team and a company. If a company is running at a loss then it is deficient and overly yin. Some yang activity will be required to address this, stem the leaks and generate more value from the collective efforts.

If on the other hand a company is excessively profitable then it attracts greater taxation, creates greater incentives for competitors to enter the market or could be because the true costs are not being measured. Perhaps the company is extracting excessive profits from its customers or from the environment. Either way this will eventually lead to a backlash and a re-dressing of this imbalance.

Where a company is making excessive profits, this yang excess can be reinvested in more nurturing yin ways to ensure that a dynamic and sustainable growth path is being followed. This could be by putting money into learning and development, succession planning or graduate training programmes. It could be by investing in a new building or creating a more pleasant working environment or by supporting flexible working policies or well-being events.

Can You Feel It?

As a leader, the fundamental ability necessary to harness this Daoist knowledge and use it to best effect is sensitivity. Sensitivity is not often a quality that people associate with leadership and yet, the ability to sense the balance of yin and yang in a person, a relationship, a team, an organisation and the bigger environment will set you apart from others and give you an edge that guides your behaviour and decision-making on a daily basis.

To some extent, the work of Daniel Goleman and his model of emotional intelligence provides a useful starting framework for developing the required sensitivity. In his research of 3,871 senior executives, he deduced that there are six leadership styles demonstrated consistently by the very best leaders. These are *Directive, Pacesetting, Visionary, Participative, Affiliative* and *Coaching*.

Style	Description
Directive	The primary objective of the directive style is immediate compliance. This style relies on *directives* rather than *direction* and uses very little dialogue. Close monitoring is supported by negative, corrective feedback with an implied, if not explicit, threat. Efforts to motivate are focussed mainly on the consequences of non-compliance.
Visionary	The *Visionary* style provides long-term direction and vision. This style relies on dialogue with others as well as the manager's unique perspective on the business to establish a vision. The manager keeps others engaged by assuring them that the direction is in the long-term best interests of the group and the organisation, and by monitoring performance toward the established goals with balanced feedback to employees.
Affiliative	The primary objective of the *Affiliative* style is to create harmony and avoid conflict. A manager utilising the *Affiliative* style spends a lot of time cultivating relationships with employees. This style tends to reward personal characteristics and avoid performance-related confrontations.
Participative	The primary objective of the *Participative* style is to build commitment through consensus. This style relies on the ability of team members to establish their own direction and to resolve their conflicts constructively. It is typically characterised by a lot of meetings, a lot of listening, recognition of adequate performance, and little criticism of low performance.

Pacesetting	The primary focus of the *Pacesetting* style is task accomplishment to high standards of excellence. Leaders utilising the *Pacesetting* style tend to lead by modelling. They establish themselves as the standard and are apprehensive about delegating. Their concern with the immediate task accomplishment makes them disinclined to collaborate with their peers, except when they need to obtain or exchange resources.
Coaching	The primary objective of the *Coaching* style is the long-term development of others. A manager using the *Coaching* style helps individuals identify their unique strengths and weaknesses. This typically involves sitting down with the employee and conducting a candid, mutual assessment of the employee's strengths and weaknesses in light of his or her aspirations. The manager helps the employee to establish a development plan, and provides ongoing support and feedback.

Reproduced with permission of Korn Ferry/Hay Group

It is possible to view each of these styles on a continuum from yin to yang with three styles that are predominantly yang and three that are predominantly yin.

The *Directive* style with the reliance on telling others what to do and even how to do it is the most yang approach.

Slightly less yang is the *Pacesetting* style. This is a highly active style of leadership where the leader sets the pace and expects everyone else to keep up.

The least yang of these three is the *Visionary* style. Although this style involves dialogue, it is primarily the leader setting out their vision in an attempt to motivate others to do their bidding.

Moving on to the more yin styles, we can start with the *Participative* style. Although the leader often maintains control and has the final say in decision-making, there is an attempt to listen to others and nurture their contributions.

The next most yin style is the *Affiliative* approach. This is very much about creating harmony in working relationships and looking after the well-being of everyone in the organisation.

The final approach is the *Coaching* style of leadership, which focusses even more intently on nurturing the development of each individual and tending to their specific needs for growth.

Greater Yin
Coaching

Affiliative

Visionary

Participative

Pacesetting

Greater Yang
Directive

So What?

Daoists are very practical and constantly test the theory in the real world. How could you use this information to improve your leadership?

A very quick and simple way is to think of a work challenge or opportunity and then ask, *"Is this a more yin or a more yang issue?"* Don't worry whether you get this right, just go with your gut feeling. Yin or Yang?

Now, consider…

- What would be 3-5 different things you could do that would be taking a yang approach to this?

Write a list and then consider…

- What would be 3-5 different things you could do that would be taking a more yin approach? List these out too.

The very act of considering things from both a yin and a yang perspective will start to increase your sensitivity to these two energies. You will also have six to ten different options for approaching this situation.

You can now get going immediately (take a yang approach) or reflect further and wait until the time is right to put one of your strategies into motion (a more yin approach). Choose which feels most appropriate.

This is your new barometer for assessing various situations and relationships. It gives you a new way of thinking and choosing the best way forward. The more you use it, the more sensitive you become and the more flexibility you bring to your leadership style that will get results in a more harmonious and sustainable way.

The best leaders are those their people hardly know exist.

The next best is a leader who is loved and praised.

Next comes the one who is feared.

The worst one is the leader that is despised …

The best leaders value their words, and use them sparingly.

When they have accomplished their task,

the people say, "Amazing!

We did it, all by ourselves!"

Lao Tzu, Tao Te Ching (Chapter 17)

Ben Green has been apprentice to a Daoist master for over 20 years. He has been teaching *Tai Chi, Daoist Yoga* and *Hand of the Wind Kung Fu* for over fifteen years in community classes as well as corporate settings.

He is an Executive Leadership and Life Coach and author of the best-selling book *Lead with Confidence – A Guide for Newly Promoted Senior Managers* as well as co-author of the soon to be published *A Doaist Path To The Life You Want.*

Ben has a real passion for helping people bring more energy into their life so they can confidently lead the life they want to lead.

He lives with his girlfriend and son in either Leeds or the Canary Islands (depending on the weather).

You can connect with Ben and discover more about his unique approach to leadership and personal development at:

Web   *ben-green.co.uk* and *lishi.org/leeds*

LinkedIn   *linkedin.com/in/1bengreen*

Please search *Facebook, Twitter* and *Instagram* for *BenGreenCoaching LeadwithConfidence* and *LishiLeedsTaiChi*

Chakra Meditation and The Power Within

Padma Coram

Most of us have grown up being taught seeing is believing.

With this deeply ingrained in our thought process we desperately work to prove our worthiness through physical and material means. Our *bucket list* usually has the boats, the houses, the *Jimmy Choos*, the *Armani* suits, the biggest office, the number of employees we have, the next destination experience, everything that helps us appear amazing, to prove we have arrived which helps us momentarily feel powerful within. We neglect the importance of things we cannot see like feelings and emotions.

True power is found in the invisible. From the emotions that rule our daily lives, to the air that we breathe, it is abundantly clear that what we cannot see is what is truly invaluable. There is no point lying in the most expensive coffin from a broken heart. This is a fatal blow to our current human understanding.

We require a solution, which resonates with our being, a solution that help revitalise our relationship with the invisible and the invaluable. Whilst there is no *Instagram* answer on how to combine the inner and outer fitness, there are some things, which we can do as first steps. Using *Chakra Meditation* is one of them. This meditation works on every level for every individual, of all walks of life and helps us with the process of going from the basic desires to gaining true personal leadership.

The seven main Chakras

The word *chakra* in Sanskrit language, literally means *wheel* or *disk*. Chakras are centres of potent power in the human body and appear as swirls of energy which balance, store and distribute the positive life-force all through our physical body along the subtle body.

Even though Indian in origin *chakra* is practiced in many cultures and countries to heal emotional issues, for physical fitness - medical system for perfect health and wellbeing, for spiritual growth, and by some cultures to help us achieve material success.

The life-force or chakras assist in the running of our body, mind and soul. If a chakra is not performing seamlessly and smoothly, it could cause our physical, mental, and spiritual health to struggle or suffer. Although there are hundreds of chakra tributaries or touch points in our body as used by acupuncturists and reflexologists we will be talking about the seven main power chakras below.

These chakras start at the base of the spine and move upwards to the last one at the crown of the head. They travel along the spinal cord of the major nerve ganglia in our physical body. This prompts us to sit straight during meditation in order to allow the chakras to function efficiently.

7. Sahasrara - Crown

6. Ajna - Third Eye

4. Vishuddha - Throat

4. Anahata - Heart

3. Manipura - Solar Plexus

2. Svadhisthana - Sacral

1. Muladhhara - Base

Chakra 1 - Muladhara Chakra - Base - I Am

The root chakra, *Muladhara,* is located at the base of the spine. It governs your most basic survival needs. When this chakra is clear and energy flows through it freely, we feel safe, secure and confident that we can easily fulfil our basic needs.

However, a blockage in this area can cause us to feel anxious and worried. Listening to signals you get from your physical and emotional body is vital. Such sensations in your body from the chakra are either comfortable or uncomfortable and your body may decide what is safe or not. As a result, this first chakra is essential in helping you to obtain security.

My Client Experience

F came to me for de-stress, confidence and clarity in decision-making sessions. He works in three different time zones in a week, and abides by the philosophy of work hard, play hard. Working odd hours, rounds of golf and the drinking hard into the morning is de rigueur. He claimed his back pain, his workload, his constant travel and the fact he no longer found his model-wife attractive, prohibited him on working on his marriage.

When I probed further, he admitted that he was constantly concerned about money and that if he divorced her, he may lose his homes and social standing.

These security issues were a base chakra blockage that urgently needed fixing. Feeling desperate he was open to meditation. We worked on all the chakras with great emphasis on the base chakra. Within seven weeks of meditation, he found the solutions to his marriage, health and work.

Within six months he reached his ideal weight, and his wife became his biggest asset in the social side of his business and they now travel mostly together and happily. *F* continues to practice the chakra mediation.

Chakra 2 -Svadhistana Chakra - Sacral - I Feel

The second chakra, *Svadhishtana* is associated with creativity in all its expressions. Located in the area of your sexual organs, the energy of this centre can be used for biological reproduction. Through focusing on this chakra creative thought processes get ignited, in your personal and business life.

This creativity draws upon the raw material of every day life and converts into something new, much like a poet using the same words you and I use daily in a different way, to create poetry that stirs something within us. The solutions to problems you face become clear to you when focusing on this chakra and you are able to access a deeper level of creativity locked in the inner chambers of your mind.

Chakra 3 - Manipura Chakra - Solar Plexus - I Do

The energy chakra, *Manipura*, is localised in your solar plexus. It's the seat of will power and self-confidence in the world. When this centre is open and flowing, you are capable of translating your intentions and desires into realities (manifest), however, when blocked you are rendered frustrated and feel impotent.

The *Law of Intention and Desire* govern the third chakra. Focusing on the third chakra you can allow the desires to fruition. If this chakra is blocked the gut feel could be cloudy and we can make wrong decisions.

I have used this chakra meditation in many areas of my life

with astonishing results. Starting my current business, writing this book is a direct result of working on this chakra.

Chakra 4 -Anahata Chakra - Heart- I Love

The fourth chakra, *Anahata*, or the heart chakra represents the unifying energy of love, kindness and compassion. It is found at the centre of the chest. When this is blocked there is a sense of otherness and one feels an alienation from ones friends and loved ones. However, when we open the chakra, it facilitates a deep connection to all beings in your life.

The law of giving and receiving governs this chakra. Love and compassion can operate in many different forms. For example, the love between a mother and child, or two partners is different, yet both feel complete. This partnership of a loving give and take is vital for the success of our personal and professional life.

My Client Experience

M had *Stage 4 Breast Cancer*, and had been told she had approximately six months to live.

M was the CEO of a large company. She appeared very stern, regimental and all-powerful in a black suit. It was difficult to reconcile the potency of the cancer she faced against her hard-as-nails exterior.

When I asked her to put aside the pen and paper she carried, and instead just speak about her emotions and love life, she was confused and saw no purpose in this exercise.

But within four hours we managed to learn how hurt she was, how unwanted and ugly she felt, causing her to be embarrassed to be a woman. We worked to unblock her heart and solar plexus chakra.

M is now not only alive but thriving. For the first time in many years she feels totally feminine, takes vacations, and is celebrating her life with deep loving connections to those around her. This has made her business grow bigger as she is now so much more approachable. She has found inner-peace and is unashamedly feminine, in a man's world, as she puts it.

Chakra 5 -Vishuddha Chakra - Throat - I Speak

The throat chakra, *Vishuddha*, is the centre of expression. When the fifth chakra is open and flowing, you have the confidence that you are capable of communicating your needs. When the fifth chakra is obstructed, a person will often feel that they are not being heard. In order to feel alive and empowered, it's important that this energy centre is clear.

The *Law of Detachment* governs the throat chakra. When opened this chakra enables you to express your truth with empathy without concern for censors or critics. Anxiety over how people will react to your views does not arise when energy is flowing freely through the chakra of expression. This chakra helps you share your truth with humility and bravely, with pride.

My Client Experience
P is a good example of how the fifth chakra works. She came to me feeling drained, hurt and stuck. She had a sensitive stomach, and constant headaches. Looking at her, one would never believe this - she was stunningly beautiful, and appeared strong and confident.

When we spoke I discovered she was just divorced, and was staying with her family. Her family has traditional values, where dating was frowned upon. She felt suffocated by all the restrictions that surrounded her.

I taught *P* the body scan meditation and we soon discovered that her throat chakra, her solar plexus and her third eye was completely blocked. Being reticent by nature she was unsure what she wanted to do with her life. However, creating an abundant income whilst maintaining her dignity was important for her. The blocked chakras created anger issues, as she could not share the truth of how she felt after her divorce. Within weeks of meditating, *P* had a breakthrough. Her *IBS* and headaches had dramatically reduced. *P* became more outgoing and felt brave enough to be more authentic and now shares her story, with no shame attached. She went on to study law specialising in womens' rights striving to help others in similar situations.

Chakra 6 - Ajna Chakra - Third Eye - I See

The intuition chakra, *Ajna*, is located in the forehead. It is the centre of wisdom, insight and intuition. When this centre is open, you have a deep sense of connection to your inner voice granting you clear life choices. When blocked, there is a sense of self-doubt and distrust. The opening of this chakra is usually associated with a clear sense of connection to ones purpose in life. The *Law of Cause and Effect* governs the sixth chakra. The voice of wisdom guides you to share the best you to manifest your full potential. This chakra helps you find the voice of your own soul and calm your inner turbulence to understand who you truly are.

My Client Experience

T was a very prominent CEO of an international company working to very tight deadlines under immense pressure.

Being very familiar with mindfulness we quickly realised that the problem actually lay at home and in his personal life, where he would agree and say *Yes* to keep the peace. He meditated intensely, especially on his third eye chakra.

Within a week he had a breakthrough on the home front, and signed a multi-billion dollar which got him the approval of his peers and the public. He continues to work internationally and has signed several multi-billion dollar deals since.

Chakra 7 - Sahasrara Chakra - Crown - I Understand

The conscious awareness chakra, *Sahasrara,* is visualised as a 1000 petaled lotus flower, at the crown of the head. When the lotus unfolds its petals, abundance is restored. Abundance and Wholeness is the union of the mind and the body – the unity of actions to create a whole healthy individual.

When your roots are receiving nourishment from the earth in the first chakra, your creative juices are flowing in the second, your intentions are empowered in the third, your heart is open and exchanging love with those around you in the fourth, you are spontaneously expressing your highest self in the fifth, you are in touch with your inner voice in the sixth, only then, does energy move into the crown chakra and you remember your essential nature as infinite, boundless and blissful.

The thousand-petal lotus flower unfolds and you know yourself as an invisible powerful spirit in a visible body and mind.

In conclusion, chakras are foundational to the relationship between our spirit and ourselves.

Chakras represent the centres of power within our body, and through chakra meditation we can overcome most obstacles be it physical, emotional, mental, material, financial or spiritual.

References

- Excerpts from the subtexts: Rig Veda

- D. Chopra, *'What everyone needs to know about their chakras'*, December 11, 2013, https://www.mindbodygreen.com/0-11943/what-everyone-needs-to-know-about-their-chakras.html (accessed 9 August 2017)

-

Indian born, **Padma Coram** is an Entrepreneur, and a Mindfulness, Meditation and Chakra specialist who helps individuals and corporates maximise their potential.

She transitioned from her professional life in the travel, music, and events industry in the Middle East to Wellness. With several awards and firsts under her belt well-travelled Padma has lived with the monks in the Himalayas, worked with Mother Theresa and Deepak Chopra, amongst others. She currently resides in London, UK and hosts private and group sessions, workshops, talks, in-person and online.

'Padma is the best combination of the East and West. She is authentic, proactive and a champion." Deepak Chopra.

Phone	*+44 (0) 2034 577 127*
Web	*www.padma.live*
Email	*office@padma.live*

Best-Practice

Performance, productivity, efficacy, effectiveness, efficiency, fast-tracking, current best thinking, compliance, governance, due diligence

There *is* an 'Individual' in team: How to Build a Team of Leaders

David Sammel

In 1990, I became head coach of a large indoor tennis club, where I got bogged down with petty problems that beset the programme. It was a large programme consisting of 600 juniors per week, 1000 adult members, ten full time and 14-part time coaches, gym staff and a pro shop to manage.

I was young, confident and hot off the tour. Besides I had been reading a lot about leadership, attended seminars of gurus such as Stephen Covey, Anthony Robbins, Wayne Dyer and others so I was convinced I could create a fantastic team. Theory without experience is well meaning but can be a disaster.

I would set a weekly meeting of two hours where we would take care of general issues and then spend time planning and growing as a team. Easy and everyone would love me!

A fractured team

Reality hit hard. The more I tried in these meetings to meet the individual needs and get a consensus among the coaches, the worse things seemed to get. The bigger goals for the programme and ideals of building a team were totally buried by the bickering and immediacy of solving each coach's perceived problems. The team began to fracture into cliques and once this happened there was no hope of becoming a united group. This was difficult to handle, because I felt that I was more than reasonable and willing to listen and learn, to include them in the decision making and encourage a mind-set of doing things for the greater good.

I had a reward system in place for good work, which also became a source of aggravation, as there was little gratitude or better cooperation.

After an award I was accused behind my back of favouritism. Where was I going wrong? I tried a few nights out and outings to help bond the team together. Imagine my disappointment when things seemed to go so well during an outing, with everyone getting on and having a good time when competing at bowls or football, yet all this camaraderie disappeared when we were back at work.

What makes a good leader?

- Vision
- Inspirational and motivating
- Good communicator
- Empathy
- Skills
- Charisma

Experience: My way or the highway

I was failing and had to change. All this new-age philosophy about listening and bringing people with you, appreciating each person's talents and nurturing a friendly environment without fear to speak out was rubbish.

What was needed was good old-fashioned discipline and strong autocratic leadership. So, I brought in a load of rules. No more freedom to express, just obey the rules and do the job or you could leave.

I had probably inherited and hired the wrong people, so if a few left, great, because then I could bring in coaches who would understand the way things worked from the start and would not bitch and sulk at the new rules.

Meetings became easier. We would tidy up everyday issues and I would discipline anyone who stepped out of line through a system of fines. I was not popular and morale was not high but at least on the surface things were more efficient and everyone was more careful with their moans. It might not have been fun or overly productive given that no one did anything extra, but at least the squabbling went underground and my bosses were happier with tried and tested methods.

Yet I was unhappy because my instincts told me that this was the wrong way, but the other way had failed. I also knew that although some staff were not the right people, others were good at their jobs and it was a mystery to me why I had failed to get their full support before the clampdown.

Even worse, these were the coaches who were leaving when the right opportunities arose.

Good teams and bad teams

My first clue as to what had gone wrong came when I thought about my relationships with players. The bonds were strong, the trust levels high and there was enthusiasm to work hard to achieve goals. I was good one-on-one. I inspired belief and confidence in individuals.

My strength was taking complex issues and making them simple to understand. The amazing thing was that the squad of players I worked with were a good team.

They supported and encouraged each other, enjoying any success that was achieved by anyone in the team.

Was it because they were young? Was it because they all had a common goal to be better players, which overcame most differences?

I knew these were not the reasons, because I had been in a college team that was fractious even though we had a common goal. Morale was not high and apart from the personal gain from the team doing well, we were quite happy to see most others on the team lose. We did well but did not achieve as much as we should have because we had not been a close team, just a team of good individuals. The leadership of the coach was poor and subject to the whims of his mood.

Good coaching

The college experience influenced the way I approach my coaching. I make sure I am emotionally stable every day.

My philosophy is to be firm but fair and to always communicate clearly what I expect from players given the level of their ambitions, which we decide together.

I have no rules apart from bringing a good attitude.

If a player fails to bring the right attitude, I calmly ask them to leave and come back when he or she is ready. The minimum gap is five minutes before the player can return. Players can opt to leave for the day or a full session.

When the player returns, I re-integrate them into the session with no fuss or discussion. I've yet to have a player return to a session and display a poor attitude again, because the decision to return and be ready is entirely theirs.

Why was the team spirit so strong with players yet seemingly impossible to recreate with staff? Why was the small team of three coaches and a trainer working with the performance players so tight knit yet in the wider group, unable to duplicate the dynamics of good teamwork? We decided it was because we were like-minded and the rest did not understand teamwork. I believed this for a while, but still it niggled me because fundamentally I knew it was not true. It took a long process of trial and error before I could claim to know the secret of creating a true team and a culture of excellence.

Building a team (of leaders)

The tennis centre was sold so the job ended.

I had increasingly been travelling with pro players and beginning to perfect the team dynamics around a player. This usually consisted of a physical trainer, medical staff, an agent, possible partner and parents. I continued to read psychology, philosophy, study leadership and motivational gurus.

Years later, I built fantastic teams, continue to advise teams and become extremely clear about the process. I will categorically argue that the worst idea is that teams are built through meetings, outings, seminars, challenges or any pursuit together. These activities lead to teamwork to solve the challenge of that day, but make little difference to the workplace unless you first meet each person individually.

In large organisations, the key managers will meet their team members individually so the process filters across the organisation. I would encourage any CEO/Leader, over time, to make the effort to engage privately with each or as many employees as possible even if only for a few minutes. It's amazing what this personal touch does for morale and culture.

Key questions for a first meeting with team members (who are tasked to prepare answers) are:

• *What is your ambition both in this job and personally?*

It's important to let staff know you are interested in them as people.

- *Summarise your job into a maximum of two bullet points, and explain how your job adds value to the team and business?*

Gain knowledge of levels of expertise and who understands or can do their job. This flushes out training requirements or poor staff.

- *If you could change one thing to make your job better what would it be?*

Any reasonable request that clearly will improve things, promise to implement immediately and be good to your word. Nothing builds trust, validates or inspires people more than being listened to and seeing ideas implemented.

- *What is the vision of this team / business as you understand it?*

It soon becomes apparent if there is any clarity or consistency on a shared vision/plan.

Follow-up meeting

Modify your vision from the information gained and arrange a follow-up meeting. In this meeting outline the vision and your ambitions for the team. Explain your philosophy and how you see them playing their part in delivering the vision they helped formulate.

Ask the question:

- *Are you comfortable playing your part and willing to accept the trust that I'm placing in you to deliver?*

Emphasise that your interest is in the results, not in telling them how to achieve them, but prefer to trust them and their experience to find the best ways to accomplish goals. Make it clear you are there to help, but have every confidence in their ability to do their job. Ensure you both know what has been agreed, and that it is a true reflection of expectations.

Once the second meeting has happened, the group meetings will become productive. Everyone will be clear about their role and on board. The meetings take on a collaborative feel where each person is focused on the task of achieving the vision and has the freedom to be honest in discussions because everyone becomes solution-minded to succeed.

Team of leaders

It is imperative that everyone is supportive in the team and that each person sees himself or herself as a leader. This does not mean that everybody is a chief.

My definition of a team of leaders is a group of people who look to support team mates when they drop the ball, and work hard to prevent any failure and genuinely want to achieve the vision that they all signed up to and agreed to deliver.

As the overall leader of the team it is important to accentuate the value in being brave and trying new ways of doing things, to think through ideas and the implications for others, and then go for it. It is impossible to evolve without experimenting and many a good idea may well turn out to be rubbish.

Help them understand that life is messy and it is not the job to create a perfectly ordered system where nothing goes wrong. The trick is to negotiate a sensible path through the unpredictable, anticipate and innovate new ways forward.

True delegation

This is the real test of management. If you trust someone to do a job then let them do it without supervision. Agree the deadline then leave them to it. Don't manage them through it or get involved unless they ask for help.

Many managers cannot resist wanting staff to accomplish tasks in the way that they would go about it —

showing or explaining how best to go about it — and inadvertently disempowering and invalidating the employee.

True delegation is freedom from the stress of being semi-responsible for tasks rather than being responsible for the outcomes.

Good delegation builds individuals' confidence and therefore the confidence of the team, as individuals stop trying to throw the ball back to you or others and begin to relish the freedom to perform.

This mind-set needs to permeate down through the team so that everyone delegates appropriately and trusts others to deliver. As the leader, your job is to lead from behind, which means observing, being available for advice and making sure that a fair balance of work is achieved.

Leadership

I will reiterate that life is messy and no matter how good your leadership skills become or how well you delegate and trust, challenges and issues will still arise. However, the magic of forming a team through the individual is beyond anything I could have imagined. Team spirit at every level grows and it is fun working with colleagues who are genuinely not scared to voice strong opinions, yet put their strength behind any action that the group or you as leader have decided is best.

The buck stops with you, so there are times when you must be strong and explain that a task or operation needs to be done a certain way because you are positive through experience that it is the right way. The team will trust your judgement if you have always followed through on delivering on an idea or change that you agreed.

The individual meetings must remain quarterly in the first year then no less than half yearly. Prepare a challenging question or two for every meeting and use them to explain the next steps and to discuss or sell evolution of the programme. It is only in these meetings that most will open and speak freely, if you never betray their confidentiality. Never divulge information to another or the group without the individual's permission.

Creating a winning team

Finally, here are few key points about the reality of leadership and creating a winning team culture:

- The time and energy needed at the start of this process means it takes far longer than either the team-meeting or *my way or the highway* approaches.

- Having the ongoing energy to inspire is challenging, especially during times when results are difficult and the goals seem impossible to achieve. However, the rewards are awesome as the team grows in confidence and strength.

- This approach takes longer, but long term it builds a legacy and produces a healthy line of succession.

- The environment and culture is one of honesty and integrity and therefore mentally healthy and a fun place to work. Again, it takes vigilance to prevent the laziness of *telling* and *unfair expectations* creeping into the programme or company.

- Everyone is emotionally invested in the success of projects.

- Extroverts can drown out the more reserved. Giving the shy ones a voice is important, as is managing the disappointment of the loud ones when the group does not submit to their enthusiasm for an idea. Over time these vastly different groups begin to merge towards each other and respect what each brings to the table.

- Hold your hands up when you are wrong. The message must remain clear that if the programme or company is constantly evolving then mistakes are part of the process, including your mistakes.

A group never reaches the place where it can stand still for long and whether we like it or not the next challenge will present itself regardless.

David Sammel is a consultant in leadership, the author of *Locker Room Power* and the coach of leading British tennis players Liam Broady and Samantha Murray and Top 20 doubles team Marcus Daniell and Marcelo Demoliner.

| Web | *https://www.lockerroompower.com* |
| Twitter | *https://twitter.com/DaveSammel* |

Ten Things I Wish I'd Known
Before I Became a Leader

Hilary McGowan

Congratulations; you've won your dream job, got promotion, and now you're a leader!

So, what happens now? However much training you've had to prepare you for this role, and you may not have had much or any which is directly relevant, you must deliver. You may be radically different from your predecessor – in age, experience, background – or you may superficially be very similar; either way, much will be expected of you by your bosses, the Board – and your staff. Experience of leadership helps make you a better leader but where do you start?

Here are ten things that I had to learn the hard way when I became a manager at the tender age of 26. With over 45 staff looking to me to lead them, and 850,000 visitors per year, depending on my staff to ensure they had a great day out and great value for money, the pressure on me to perform did not hit me until my first day in the job. Why should it have done? It was my dream job – running *York Castle Museum*, the museum with the street, in one of the most historic cities in the world.

It would be enjoyable, stimulating and fun.

But I learnt more in the next five years than anyone could have expected; here's what I learnt.

Lead, not do; inspire not tell

Leadership is vital so make time to be strategic as it is too easy to get swallowed up by the day-to-day work which should be the responsibility of your staff. Details are safe for you but they are not the preserve of leaders.

You may feel more comfortable messing around *in the weeds* on the forest floor (it's where you used to be after all) but a leader should be scanning the horizon above the tree canopy. Your foot soldiers cannot see this view but it is the leader's role to look higher and further, and to interpret what you see.

Lead, not do – you have staff to do the doing – and inspire, not tell – if they believe, they will get on and achieve.

Your role as a leader is to inspire hope for a better future.

Don't be afraid to hire people better than you

Mark McCormack, the founder of *International Management Group (IMG)* - and author of *What they don't teach you at Harvard Business School,* (1984) - always knew that others would be better than him at some things, so if he hired them, he could learn from them too and they would help him to progress the innovation he was seeking.

Don't be afraid of not being able to control what these people do as they should be a vital catalyst in your change programme. When I first did this, the individual I appointed became a key person in my drive to transform the organisation.

He was responsible for marketing, creating new income through attracting new audiences for our temporary exhibitions programme. He stretched my leadership and I learnt a lot about managing challenging mavericks. But I gave him his head and I achieved radical change much faster and more effectively than I would have done without him.

Three years down the line, he left; he had always moved on

rapidly as he loved a new challenge. I was happy with this as he had helped me effect lasting change and we were better and stronger as a result of his disruptive innovation.

Be visible

You cannot be seen too often so spend time talking to and listening to people: practice *Management By Walking About (MBWA)*. Staff will get used to this but initially it will make them nervous unless your predecessor did it too.

Getting used to seeing you out and about makes it easier for them to approach you about an idea or a delicate problem. You must also get used to them stopping talking when you walk past them at the end of the corridor or enter a room; if you get paranoid about what they're saying about you, you'll never be a successful leader. Most of the time, they will be talking about something else. But if one or two of them come to you to talk quietly, you must listen.

If you are in a public-facing business (like I was in museums), then being seen by the *Front-of-House (FoH)* staff (or whatever you call them) and the public, is even more important. And by watching, you will learn how your business interacts with your customers and users.

When I ran *York Castle Museum*, we had 850,000 visitors per year, so huge numbers to manage in two Georgian buildings with lots of corridors and bottle necks. Tempers could easily fray when it was very busy with lots of families, so being seen was often vital to support the *FoH* staff. If problems arise, people demand to see the duty manager; if that's you (and it often was me) then you can calm the situation much more effectively if you are familiar with how your site/business looks and what problems it has when it's busy. If you're not out and about much, then you won't understand the problems your staff and your customers encounter.

In addition, if your staff know they can rely on you to support them, they will respond more positively when you suggest that changes in their behaviour may reduce the numbers of problems in future. Encourage them to learn from how you handle them and take the heat out of the situation.

Be generous in your praise

You should never shy away from praising a job well done or saying thank you. Some people hesitate to offer praise and many struggle to take it. This should not stop you offering it but ensure that it is deserved and don't scatter compliments like confetti or they become meaningless. So always mean what you say, and that is a good mantra for life in general, not just for leaders.

Paying someone a compliment will also give you an opportunity to help your staff to accept compliments.

The British in particular are very poor at this and just shrug them off with comments like *it was nothing really, I couldn't have done it without my team* or *Oh, this old thing?!*

Accepting compliments and thanks with a good grace is a sign of maturity and self confidence, so encouraging your staff to say *thank you* and smile at the giver; this is a developmental goal for many.

You may be surprised at how difficult some people find this.

Tell the truth faster

On the more negative side of leadership, you must never hesitate to tell someone the painful truth about their performance or behaviour, if it's needed.

I have had to sack people, suspend them for sexual misconduct and judge complaints, so developing a way of coping with the pressures these bring is essential if you are to be an effective leader. Ensuring you know what your procedures are and where the boundaries of your authority lie are fundamental but also be aware of what you are saying and how, and make yourself feel confident enough not to fill silence with speech.

This is a natural human reaction under pressure but if you are a leader, then less can be more.

Take a deep breath and just do it.

Lead through highs and lows

Morale is low: it always is, according to many workers. This does not equate to disliking your job, but is a shared view often amongst staff of lesser abilities, not those high flyers whom you may warm to more naturally.

Leading the ordinary Joe or Josephine day in, day out, is the real challenge of leadership. We tend to spend most time on those who are easy to manage and to lead, but those *ordinary* staff who need more encouragement are those who can be most productive and who can be relied upon to underpin the organisation on a longer term basis.

Human beings cannot exist in a constant state of euphoria and the highs and lows of normal business are part of working life. Leading your staff through the low points is perhaps what you expect as a new leader, but leading them through and beyond a major success is a true test of leadership.

Managing their descent from exhilaration is a challenge for anyone but it's essential if you need them to get back on track and be productive as soon as possible.

So if someone tells you that morale is low, don't worry, good leadership should prevent this becoming an endemic problem.

Follow your instincts

You must always rely on your instincts to ensure you don't get pushed around. When I was persuaded not to follow my instincts, by a senior manager or by my boss, it always ended in tears.

Having been instructed to appoint someone I did not wish to appoint on two occasions, I never again allowed myself to be persuaded if my instincts told me otherwise (both appointments were not successful).

Stand up for what you know to be true and right for your organisation, and for you. You will also earn respect as you continue to be seen to have made the right decisions. If you feel you do not have strong instincts, just listen more carefully to yourself so you can develop them.

Be decisive

You will need to cultivate your own mantras to aid decisive decision making: you cannot be seen to be vacillating.

So when in doubt you can ask yourself, for example: *"What would Andrew Priestley/Dan Priestley/Richard Branson/Stephen Covey do?"*

And while you are thinking about this, ask your member of staff, *"If I wasn't here to ask, what would you do? what do you think?"* Then ask them open questions to help them analyse their options so they can come to their own decisions, not always asking you.

Them relying on you for answers is not leadership, as a leader is not leading if they are simply issuing orders (unless you are on the battlefield).

These are very powerful development tools to use as they help any member of your staff to improve their analysis of a problem, their decision-making and grow as a result.

Disregard Armchair Critics

MCC Syndrome: Marylebone Cricket Club, which owns *Lords*, is the body which creates and upholds the *Laws and Rules of Cricket*. The Members in the Pavilion always think they could lead England more effectively than the Captain out on the cricket field, so accept that staff will think this too and consequently be a real challenge to manage.

If they are passionate about their work or the organisation's mission, if they are intelligent and experienced, so they will think they can do your job better than you.

Accept this and get on with your real job.

Hilary McGowan works with museum and heritage organisations to help them stand on their own two feet, be stronger and survive into the future.

She has worked in the *cultural sector* for over 30 years, some of that time as a museums and arts director in York, Exeter and Bristol, and for the last 20 years, she has run her own successful business.

As she was known for turning museums round, making them more customer-focused and more profitable, this became the focus of her business. She is a *Trustee of Bletchley Park*, the site of the WWII code breakers. She is now a leading authority on organisational development and governance in the cultural sector.

Web	*http://www.hilarymcgowan.co.uk*
Twitter	*@HilaryMcGowan*

Emerging Trends

**Innovation, disruption, new thinking,
gaps in the market, emerging industries,
emerging trends, transitions, transformations**

Why Great Leaders Need To Be Great Storytellers

Susan Payton

*"The most powerful person in the world is the storyteller.
The storyteller sets the vision, values and agenda
of an entire generation that is to come." – Steve Jobs*

Hitting the *publish* button to send my personal story *out there* into the world, felt like one of the most uncomfortable things I'd ever done. *"What have you done?"* screeched the voice in my head, *"Why did you do that? No-one wants to hear your story. Why would they? They're busy. Who cares? How embarrassing".*

As the panic began to rise in my body, an email pinged into my inbox. I gingerly opened it and, as I started to read it, a lump formed in my throat. It was from someone thanking me for my honesty and saying how inspired they were by my story. They went on to share a bit about the challenges they were facing themselves and I was touched that they had trusted me to be their confidante.

A couple of minutes later I got another one. Along the same lines. And then another. And so it continued. For days!

I quickly realised that being so open about my less-than-perfect journey had meant that people could relate to me. People could resonate with my story.

Many felt compelled to contact me, because my story was like theirs, and some wanted to work with me - because of how my story had made them *feel*.

And my biggest realisation of all? That telling my story was never actually about me. It was about who my story had touched, how it had helped and inspired them and the bond that had been created.

It was this realisation that fired up my passion for bringing the *human* element back into business. I knew that, in a world where it is getting harder and harder to stand out from the crowd, business owners and leaders needed to step up, speak their truth, share their story and inspire their audience.

And I am not alone in my mission. The ancient art of storytelling is a hot topic in business these days, and not one that is likely to be going away any time soon.

As I write this, *HKS Inc.* - *"A team of more than 1,300 architects, interior designers, urban designers, scientists, artists, anthropologists and other professionals working together across industries and across the globe"* are recruiting for a *Storyteller*.

Etsy recently advertised for someone *"who can breathe life into the stories about our unique brand and mission on a global scale".*

And big brands including *Microsoft, Apple* and *Google* have added a *Chief Storytelling Officer (CSO)* to their C-Suite.

So why the big emphasis on story?

Although *Nike* have been employing a *Storyteller* since the nineties, others started to follow suit after something happened in 2004 that changed the world forever. *Facebook* happened!

The launch of *Facebook (2004)*, and *YouTube (2005)* a year later, had a huge impact on the way business was done on a global scale as people were able to connect and share stories with others, around the world, 24 hours a day, seven days a week.

Since then, savvy business leaders and marketers have noticed the subtle shift away from *transactional selling* to focusing on building relationships first.

Leading with story has become an integral part of that shift. With a millennial generation that is all about being part of a greater purpose, and consumers who make choices based on a brand's mission and vision, using narrative to communicate your purpose and your *why* has never been so important.

So, as a Leader, what stories should you be telling?

I don't think anyone would argue that, to make a difference in people's lives, you need to build meaningful connections first.

However, many businesses have become so focused on the what and the how, they've forgotten that people want to know why. Or they're so programmed to tell the facts and explain the function, they've forgotten that *people buy from people.*

I believe that to build trust, loyalty and long-term relationships, there are three important stories that you will want to master and tell:

Your Personal Story

"There's always room for a story that can transport people to another place." - J K Rowling

Leadership is about authenticity. People want to know the real you. Being honest and open about your journey allows others to understand and engage with the *essence* of who you are, why you are here and where you are going.

Sharing your highs and lows, your successes and failures, your mistakes and learnings does require being OK with showing some vulnerability, but as humans we are moved by stories of courage over adversity, triumph over evil and heroes stepping up to win the day. People seek out stories that inspire them and make them feel they too could conquer and prevail.

So, whatever level of success you have now achieved, whatever mountain you have conquered, it is the story of what it took to get there that people will connect with.

What challenges you faced along the way – personally, professionally, emotionally and physically - and what got you through the tough times. What you had to do to get yourself back on track when the path was no longer clear and who guided, inspired and influenced you.

Your audience will want to learn from your foresight, reflections and realisations. They will relate your story to theirs and look for similarities. They will want to be left feeling that they too could climb their own mountain.

Richard Branson, Elon Musk, Tony Robbins, Oprah Winfrey and *Sheryl Sandberg* are great storytellers - they all tell candid stories of their journey, their successes, their failures, their learnings, philosophy, values, goals and vision.

People follow those who have a clear purpose. Those who are on a quest. Those who are here to make a difference.

If you want to inspire others and be seen as a thought leader, *start with your story.*

Your Business Story

"The story of Virgin – its ups and downs, opportunity and challenges – is what attracts people to our products and services, and also to work with us. We would be nothing without our story." – Richard Branson

Your *Why*

Taking the time to unpack and craft the story of who you are and why you do what you do is imperative for clearly communicating your mission, vision and why your business exists.

Leading with purpose and passion allows you to move away from competing, in a highly commoditised world, on features and price. As Seth Godin says, "Being a commodity provider is fine, as long as you're OK with competing in a race to the bottom".

Being clear about your *why* allows people to engage with and get excited about what you do and where your story is going. It enables those who feel aligned with your purpose to become a part of something bigger than they could ever be on their own.

Having innovative ideas and a powerful vision is great, but unless you can inspire others to buy into those ideas and that vision, it doesn't work.

As Simon Sinek points out in his book *Start With Why (2009)* very few people or companies can clearly articulate why they do what they do.

He explains, "By why I mean what is your purpose, cause or belief? Why does your company exist? Why do you get out of bed every morning? And why should anyone care?"

Your Values

Your story is your DNA and an integral part of your brand. It is the bedrock that underpins everything you say, do and stand for. Your core beliefs, how you are different and who you serve are the solid foundations that everything else sits.

Stating your values on your website is nowhere near as compelling and authentic as having them jump out of your story and be reflected in everything you do.

Flowers Unlimited Brighton understand this better than anyone. They continually surprise and delight at every stage of the customer journey. From emailing a photo to the customer of their flower arrangement being put together to posting the recipient a packet of flower food a few days later, with a note reminding them to change the water, they don't need to tell us how highly they value customer service. They show us. It's part of the story they are living and breathing every day.

Story is not just a well-crafted About page or mission statement, it is in every interaction with every customer and, ultimately, it is how others feel when they interact with you and your brand.

As Carmine Gallo, author of *The Storyteller's Secret (2016)*, says, "Storytelling is not something we do; storytelling is who we are".

Your Customer's Story

"Business, like life, is all about how you make people feel. It's that simple. And it's that hard" – Danny Meyer

Knowing your customer's story is critical.

For your story to be highly relevant and compelling to your target market, you need to be really clear to whom you're talking to.

A business consultant was asked to review the marketing for a new, luxury waterfront development, as their current marketing wasn't working. He quickly spotted where they were going wrong - their brochures were full of young, good-looking guys, standing next to flash cars with gorgeous girls on their arm.

However, when he visited another luxury waterfront development and knocked on a few doors, he discovered that the residents were (in his words) *fat, middle-aged, bald blokes, who worked hard and wanted to enjoy living somewhere nice with their wife and kids.*

A million miles from the image of the young dude on the front of the brochure. Understanding the story going on in your customer's head is key.

It is only by having a deep understanding of where they are at, where they want to be and what is stopping them from getting there, that you can demonstrate empathy, speak to your customers in a language that will resonate and show them where you fit into their story.

When you tell a compelling story, your customers will want your products to be a part of their lives.

Online software company *Help Scout* launched their *Customer Spotlight*s project when they realised the value of getting real-life, meaningful feedback from their customers about how their lives were made better for using their products. Highlighting these stories on their site reflects their brand image and the kind of customers they serve.

Only when you truly understand where your customer is at, can you paint a picture of what the life they want looks like and how you can help them achieve it.

So, What Next?

Leading by story doesn't have to mean hiring a *CSO.* Your products, services, processes, team, suppliers, market and industry will all provide a wealth of stories to help bring your business to life.

The marketing team at *Team GB* have the challenge of keeping their fans engaged for four years, between Olympic competitions! How do they do that? By consistently telling great stories. By profiling up-and-coming athletes and giving fans bite-sized chunks of sport content, they build engagement and excitement before the *Games* even start.

Look at your customer's journey and identify the stories you can engage them with along the way.

Keep It Simple

As with most things in business, there is a golden rule of effective storytelling - *Keep It Simple.*

Complex stories will confuse and likely lose your audience.

Story is never about *dumping*. It needs to be clear, concise, succinct, highly relevant and leave the audience feeling inspired to take action.

Keep the language and structure simple and uncomplicated.

A good rule of thumb is to write so that a 12-year-old could understand and engage with it.

Carmine Gallo says, "If you want to sound smart and confident, replace big words with small ones. Big words don't impress people, big words frustrate people."

Winston Churchill, whose speeches are arguably some of the most powerful, inspiring and emotive speeches of all time, kept his language simple and his sentences short.

Short, punchy stories make a bigger impact. Leadership is about motivating people with clear direction, concise messages and strong calls to action.

Getting Started

So, you get it. You get story is important. You understand the power of storytelling, but how do you get started? There are certainly people (like me) who can help you with that, but answering these questions is a great place to start:

- *Who are you and why do you do what you do?*
- *What does your business stand for and what is the difference it is here to make?*
- *What is going on for your customer and where does your business fit into their story?*

You may also want to download my free workbook at *www.fivebrandstories.com* to see how I dissect five brand stories, explain why they work and show you how to start crafting your own stories to create connection and brand loyalty.

Storytelling is here to stay

As Gallo says, "In the next 10 years, the ability to tell your story persuasively will be the single greatest skill in helping you accomplish your dreams ... the story you tell yourself and the story you share with others will unlock your potential and, quite possibly, change the world. Isn't it time you shared yours?"

Isn't it?

References

- Gallo, Carmine. (2016) *The Storyteller's Secret*
- Priestley, Daniel (2014). Key *Person of Influence*
- Sinek, Simon (2009) *Start With Why*
- *Team GB - Campaign (March 2017)*

Susan Payton is a *Story Strategist* with a background in media, events and property. Susan's world was turned upside down in 2006 when she was diagnosed with ME. The next few years saw her devoted to getting her health back on track and led to her training as an *Advanced NLP Practitioner* and *Life Coach*.

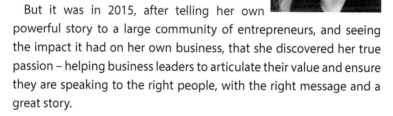

But it was in 2015, after telling her own powerful story to a large community of entrepreneurs, and seeing the impact it had on her own business, that she discovered her true passion – helping business leaders to articulate their value and ensure they are speaking to the right people, with the right message and a great story.

Web	*www.thebusinessofstories.com*
Email	*susan@thebusinessofstories.com*
Facebook	*BusinessOfStories*
Twitter	*TheBizofStories*

It's Time to Put Leadership on the To-Do List

Antoinette Oglethorpe

What's the difference between *leadership* and *management*? Does it really matter? Does anyone care?

Well yes, it seems they do. Recently, a client of mine, a CEO of a fast-growing, technology company asked me to run a session on *Leadership vs. Management* at his quarterly offsite. Inwardly I groaned thinking *"Oh no. Not this old chestnut again."* Out loud I politely said *"Yes of course. May I ask why? What would you like to happen as a result?"*

The CEO explained that the 40 people at this offsite were the most senior people in his organisation. He needed them to help him grow the organisation, realise the vision and live out their mission and values. But he saw a group of people consumed by the day to day operation. In his opinion, they spent too much time managing and not enough time leading. He was hoping this short session would help change that.

My spirits lifted. My client didn't want an academic debate about the differences between leadership and management. He wanted to change the way his people behaved so they spent more time focussed on strategic leadership. That's something I could help with.

And that's what I aim to do here, too. It will answer that age-old question: *What's the difference between leadership and management?* It will then go on to look at what current organisations need from leadership and management. Finally, it will share strategies that leaders can use to create the right balance between leadership and management.

What's the difference between leadership and management?

The glib answer you'll often get to that question is: "Leadership is doing the right things. Management is doing things right."

It's a quote from Peter Drucker. It's not wrong. But nor is it particularly helpful. So, let's turn to another management guru for more clarity.

John Kotter, professor of leadership at Harvard University defines them as follows:

"Management is a set of processes that keep an organisation functioning. They make it work today – they make it hit this quarter's numbers. The processes are about planning, budgeting, staffing, clarifying jobs, measuring performance, and problem-solving when results did not go to plan."

Leadership is very different. "It is about aligning people to the vision, that means buy-in and communication, motivation and inspiration."

In other words, management focuses on work and tasks. These activities fit within the subject of resource: human, time, money, and equipment, including:

- **Planning** – Planning resources and tasks to achieve the objectives
- **Budgeting** – Managing the constraints of budgets in the department or project
- **Organising** – Organising support and resources

- **Controlling** – Controlling the standards required to deliver the objectives
- **Coordinating** – Coordinating and directing tasks for the achievement of goals
- **Resource use** – Ensuring their team use effective resources for the task at hand
- **Time management** – Ensuring their team conduct tasks and activities within the correct time frame
- **Decision Making** – Making the right decisions in the heat of the moment
- **Problem Solving** – Ensuring their team contain and resolve problems

Leadership focuses on achieving new goals, keeping the team motivated and empowered to achieve as much as they can. It's also about getting the best out of each individual for the benefit of the team. It's about leading by example, inspiring, empowerment. It's about creating the most conducive environment for team success:

- **Vision** – Focusing on the long-term vision or goal
- **Motivation** – Motivating and empowering others to challenge the norm
- **Inspiration** – Inspiring others and injecting enthusiasm
- **Persuasion** – Persuading and influencing others to bring them along with them
- **Team work** – Encouraging effort, commitment and collaboration
- **Building Relationships** – Building strong relationships and partnerships with clients and colleagues
- **Engagement** – Listening and understanding employee's needs and aspirations

- **Development** – Coaching, encouraging and giving freedom for individuals to learn and grow
- **Mentoring** – Passing knowledge and wisdom onto the team and its individuals

How can you tell if you are *leading* or *managing?*

In his *Harvard Business Review* article *Three Differences Between Managers and Leaders,* Vineet Nayar describes three tests.

1. Counting Value vs. Creating Value

Management is about counting value by maintaining what is already established. Activities focus on watching the bottom-line, controlling workflow in the organisation and preventing any kind of chaos.

Leadership, however, focuses on creating some kind of value. It's about coming up with new ideas and kick starting the organisation's shift or transition to a forward-thinking phase. *Leadership* involves having one eye on the horizon. Activities focus on developing new techniques and strategies for the organisation. It requires immense knowledge of current trends, advancements, skillsets, and a clarity of purpose and vision.

2. Circles of Power vs. Circles of Influence

Management relies on a circle of power where action is achieved mostly through authority. Activities focus on managing and influencing the behaviour and actions of those who report to you.

Leadership on the other hand relies on a circle of influence where action is achieved mostly through persuasion. Activities focus on influencing the behaviour and actions of those over who you have no authority.

3. Managing Work vs. Leading People

Management relies on controlling a group to achieve a certain goal. *Leadership*, on the other hand, is the ability of an individual to motivate, influence, and enable other employees to make a contribution towards the success of an organisation. Inspiration and influence separate leadership from management, not control and power.

Leadership and management in today's organisations

Leadership versus management, although relatively easy to distinguish between the two, is complex because today's organisations need people to be both.

Perhaps there was a time when you could separate the requirements of a manager and a leader. A foreman in an industrial-era factory probably didn't have to give much thought to what he was producing or to the people who were producing it. His or her job was to follow orders, organise the work, assign the right people to the necessary tasks, coordinate the results, and ensure the job got done as ordered.

The focus was on *efficiency*.

But in the new economy, where value comes increasingly from the knowledge of people, and where workers are no longer undifferentiated cogs in an industrial machine, management and leadership are not easily separated. People now look to their managers, not just to assign them a task, but to define for them a purpose. And managers must organise workers, not just to maximise efficiency, but to nurture skills, develop talent and inspire results.

More than ever, in today's fast-changing world, organisations need to be *agile*. They need to be able to move quickly and easily. And that relies on having strong leadership and strong management in equal measure.

In their paper *Agility: It rhymes with stability*, McKinsey make the point that agile organisations learn to be both stable (resilient, reliable, and efficient) and dynamic (fast, nimble, and adaptive) .

The metaphor I like to use is that of a surfer. For a surfer to successfully ride the ocean waves, they need the core stability that will hold them firm and upright on the surfboard. They also need the flexibility to move, adapt and respond as the waves approach. It's the same in today's organisations. To ride the waves of change, organisations need the core stability that comes from strong management practices. They also need the dynamism and flexibility that comes from strong leadership.

It's not either/or. It's both.

Those that think it's an either/or situation, will crash out and get dumped into the metaphorical sea. Strong leadership without strong management risks chaos, reinventing the wheel and low efficiency. Strong management without strong leadership and you stifle morale, risk-taking and creativity.

Creating the balance between management and leadership

Leadership and management are like yin and yang. For every leadership activity, there is an equal and balancing management activity:

Leadership	Management
People-oriented	Task-oriented
Participative	Autocratic
Team development	Team performance
Long-term	Short-term
Change	Stability
Transformational	Transactional
Generalist	Specialist

For success in today's organisations, it's not enough to just have strong leadership skills or strong management skills. The most prized skill of all is the versatility to achieve balance between both. That means being freely able to use both sets of skills, unlimited by bias in favour of one and prejudice against the other.

In my experience, like the client I mentioned at the start of the chapter, making time for management isn't so much of an issue. The real challenge lies in making time for leadership.

And for good reason. Leadership is about the future.

It's about being proactive not reactive. And so, it falls into the category of being important but not urgent. As Charles Hummel highlighted in *Tyranny of the Urgent*, there is a regular tension between things that are urgent and things that are important—and far too often, the urgent wins.

In the business world, this means that demands of your boss, your clients, or petty office relationships can often take priority over things that matter. Things like developing a long-term strategy, inspiring and developing employees, or building collaboration in a team. The urgent, though less important, is prioritised, and so the important is put on the back burner.

So, how do you make time for leadership? Here are three suggestions:

1. Put it on the to-do list

For most business leaders, their to-do lists are full of management activities. Every task and every meeting focuses on writing proposals, delivering work, managing budgets and achieving short-term goals. As one client said to me, "When you have a month of 20% year on year growth you're scrambling. It's challenging to get away from the day to day tasks and activities and concentrate on the big picture and strategy for future growth".

With a never-ending to-do list full of management activities, it's no wonder that leadership gets squeezed out. So, it's time to put it on the to-do list or book it into the calendar. Carve out time to step away from the day to day business and work on the stuff that will grow the business. For example, developing and communicating the vision; building capacity and capability in your people; creating a culture of innovation and growth.

2. Change the agenda

Many people feel that they are leading when they spend time with others because they think they are being people-oriented. But it depends what the agenda is. If the whole conversation focuses on the operation and the day to day business, you are simply carrying out management activities in a group. When you stop discussing the tasks at hand and talk about vision, purpose, and aspirations instead, that's when you have moved into leadership. Instead of always having Operations Meetings, make sure you also have regular Strategy Meetings.

So, change the agenda. Or even better, don't have any agenda. Instead, have a powerful question. For example:

- *"What will success look like in five years?"*
- *"How can we build our profitability?"*
- *"What are the key opportunities for growth over the next 12 months?"*

3. Hire a coach

One way to carve out time for leadership and change the agenda to one that is more strategic is to get outside help in the form of a coach. A coach provides the space for leaders and leadership teams to step away from the business for a period of time and focus on strategic issues. They will make sure it happens in spite of any crises that happen to have arisen that day.

A coach will also ask the right questions to challenge the status quo and explore future possibilities.

Whether it be at an individual level or team level, coaching can provide invaluable clarity, perspective and awareness.

References

- Vineet Nayar (HBR August 2013), *Three Differences Between Managers and Leaders*
- Wouter Aghina, Aaron De Smet and Kirsten Weerda (McKinsey Quarterly December 2015), *Agility: It rhymes with stability.*
- Charles E. Hummel (1994) *Tyranny of the Urgent!*

Antoinette Oglethorpe has developed leaders for some of the most successful organisations in the world, including *P&G, Accenture* and *XL Group.*

A defining moment in her career was when she helped start up *Avanade*, a joint venture between *Accenture* and *Microsoft.*

As *International Learning Director* for *Avanade*, she played a key role in developing the people needed to build the organisation as it grew to 1200 employees in its first year.

She now runs a professional training and coaching company which specialises in developing leaders and leadership teams for fast-growth, tech organisations. Antoinette is author of *Grow Your Geeks - A Handbook for Developing Leaders in High-Tech Organisations*, available at Amazon. Learn more and connect at:

www.antoinetteoglethorpe.com.

Leaders You Can Trust:
Five Behaviours of Highly Effective Leaders

Andrew Priestley

When I started business leadership coaching in 1998 the popular thinking was: *success leaves clues.* And the idea was to model yourself on the qualities of successful leaders. If I went into a client's office they had books by high profiled authors - mostly men such as Jack Welch, Richard Branson, Lee Iacocca, Colin Powell, Warren Bennis - and occasionally - leaders like Dame Anita Roddick.

Every author had their *leadership success formula* comprising *nine Cs, four lessons, 13 pillars* or *12 strengths.*

This is not a new idea. Benjamin Franklin (1726) had whittled success down to 13 virtues; then successful character traits/qualities for leadership and life were being espoused by Isaac Watt (1821) who identified 16 traits, Ralph Waldo Emerson (1836), and notably, Samuel Smiles (1859) who coined the phrase *self-help.*

This approach to success seems to have shaped the works of Dale Carnegie (1936) and Napoleon Hill (1937) and self-development books since.

We have also had leadership training based on styles of leadership, personality and power. The result is the same.

"If I just copy the right leader and the right traits I will be successful as a leader, right?" The obvious problem is: how do you train someone to be *charismatic, confident* or *decisive,* easily or at all? We can describe those qualities but getting someone to *be* them is another issue.

I have three concerns.

Most of our leadership models come from *military, sports, politics* and *business.* My leadership model draws exclusively on *business* leaders. I only coach on what *business* leaders do.

I am yet to see business people effectively applying leadership principles from sport personalities, politicians and the military that have any lasting efficacy.

I once heard a famous rugby coach telling an enthralled room full of corporate executives the secrets to *business* success. This highly successful career-coach had never run a business. By the way, there is no *time-out* in business.

Secondly, getting advice from a corporate legend is appreciated but I am yet to meet anyone whose read Jack Welch's books who has leveraged Jack's advice. They lack Jack's life experience, knowledge or resources. Jack Welch could literally throw 50 MBAs at a problem. That's not me, the overwhelming bulk of my clients and maybe not you.

Thirdly, and critically, the assumption is simple: *who you are isn't good enough.* You need to become someone else. You need a personality bypass. I meet leaders who definitely try but end up feeling like an impostor.

I remember trying to shoehorn an executive into the qualities of *charisma, credibility* and *competence.* The coaching sessions were interesting but there was no profound transformation. In utter frustration and embarrassment I abandoned the approach of trying to teach leaders to be like someone else.

Shortly after that I started to work with leaders working in high-end compliance, life-and-limb industries where if you get it wrong, on a good day you get fined; and on a bad day someone dies.

My clients worked under high pressure where they rarely had the luxury of mistakes. Think civil aviation, environment, mining, medical and you have the picture. In working with these clients I started to notice, over time, that even given highly stringent work cultures they were still highly effective and operated calmly within those contexts.

None of my clients had the time to rush back to their office and search for what Lee Iacocca or Jack Welch would do in their situation.

The most highly effective leaders I met then - and still meet today - consistently demonstrate five core behaviours – things they are doing on a consistent basis regardless of their personality or situation. Behaviours you can observe and apply almost immediately.

- They are **aware** of what's happening around them *(situational awareness)* and critically, how they *feel* about what's happening *(response awareness);* and how they want to respond.

- They **assert** themselves. If they have an opinion they state it. Rarely are effective leaders politically correct. They are usually plainly spoken, clear and direct without finesse. The key tool seems to be scrutiny - *asking* - rather than *telling*.

- They broker clear **agreements** with others (and importantly themselves).

- They hold others (and themselves) **accountable**. They manage those agreements. They will say things like, *"Did you agree to this ... or not?*

- They reflect on what happened, what worked and what didn't and then decide if they contributed to the problems or if in fact they *were* the problem. They use that reflection to **adjust** their game.

So:

- Are you aware of what's happening and how you feel about what's happening? Are you aware of what you need to say or do?

- Are you communicating that awareness to others clearly?

- Do you know what you want (instead)? And are you asking for what you want?

- Do you get clear agreements and undertakings from others?

- Do you hold people accountable for what they agreed to do? Do you manage those agreements?

- Do you reflect on what worked and what didn't; and adjust your game? Is that working?

That's what I' see highly effective leaders *do*. The operative word here is *see*. You can *observe* these behaviours in others; and yourself. Here's an example.

I had a client - lets call her Janine, a registered medical administrator - running a critical care unit in a hospital. Janine had been promoted to the leadership role as a result of rising through the ranks. When we started Janine was struggling in a frontline leadership role.

Janine had a lot of problems but we decided to work on her top three issues. One of them was nurses arriving late for the night shift which placed an unnecessary stress on other nurses keen to hand over to the inbound nurses.

One night, two heart attacks went off simultaneously and being short of staff, one of the patients nearly died. This created a moral dilemma for the attending nurse. Which patient do I focus on?

And, technically, that is deemed an *incident* which has to be recorded and reported.

When I spoke to Janine she said she was aware that staff had been arriving late for over three months. She had tried to gently discipline the offenders without success. Because there was a nurse shortage Janine was mindful not to offend. Understand, your *regulars* get to know you and Janine's staff basically knew they could get away with arriving late without being disciplined or it being formally registered.

So, while Janine's awareness was working fine she was failing to *respond* to her awareness: i.e., do her job, assert her leadership and treat *all* late arrivals as an *incident*. She knew what she needed to do but she wasn't doing it. She was behaving incongruently.

The problem with behaving incongruently - saying one thing and doing another - is you create the very problems you are trying to avoid.

At the heart of it, Janine wanted to be liked but in this context *being liked* was too narrow a perspective.

Janine was also reinforcing the idea that her staff could arrive late; and creating a culture of diminished *duty of care*. Her self-appraisal of her leadership was self-depreciating which was feeding her lack of confidence in a leadership role.

In coaching:

- Janine ramped up her **awareness** of issues and started to formally collect problems and note especially how she was handling those issues.
- She started to **assert** what she wanted.
- She brokered clear **agreements** around shift times and change overs.
- She held her team **accountable** and managed the agreements - without exception - of repeat late comers

– which was actually a relief to committed staff. Respect went up. Basically, she asked questions like: *What exactly needs to happen to get you here on time, tomorrow?*

- Janine started to self-critique her hits and misses more closely and **adjusted** her game. Her effectiveness more positively and her confidence in the role grew.

It took about three months but the flow-on benefits to staff and patients and the tone of that ward was profound. It goes without saying that Janine dramatically mitigated or resolved pressing *duty-of-care* issues.

Janine started to trust her own awareness and respond more appropriately. She clearly asserted her expectations on a range of issues. She began to broker clear agreements - *This is what I want, do you agree?* And her ability to hold others accountable improved markedly.

Importantly, Janine's ability to reflect on her own performance and successfully adjust her game gave her greater *confidence* and *credibility* as a leader.

I know nothing about running a critical care unit, or mining, or water treatment or employment law or any other of the broad range of industries and sectors my clients come from. But when my clients focus on those five aspects - and it is frequently a challenge - I observe an uplift in leadership effectiveness.

Janine reported she, at last, felt *comfortable* and *effective* in the leadership role because finally she felt she could *be* herself.

Leaders of course must be competent, and capable. They must still have qualifications, formal skills, core competencies and experience, but the leadership focus is on doing what *feels* natural, intuitive and grounded.

It is immensely satisfying to see leaders relieved of the burden of going through the motions of leadership.

I think that's new. If not new, then remarkable.

Here are some key questions that will help you become more effective as a leader:

- What am I **aware** of? When did I *first* become **aware** there was a problem? And how do I feel about that?
- How do I want to appropriately respond to my awareness? What do I want to see happen, *instead*? What are my options? What are the implications of doing nothing?
- What do I need to say or do in this situation? What's critical to resolve?
- Do I know what I want? Do I know what *good* looks like? Can I broker clear **agreements** with others? And myself?
- Can I manage those agreements? Can I hold others **accountable** for what they agreed to do?
- Am I reflecting on what's working and what isn't? How am I contributing to what's happening? Do I need to **adjust** my game?

Obviously, the coaching relationship helps to drive the *momentum* of that leader's development. The coach holds that leader accountable. (In my own case, I get paid to figuratively *hold the leaders' feet to the fire!*)

But in my experience questions like these can be applied by anyone - right now - with great effect.

Importantly, you're not trying to be like someone else. I'm trying to leverage who I am but in a way that feels resourceful, purposeful and appropriate. (And of course, compliant.)

So what happened to Janine?

Over 6-12 months, Janine evolved into an effective leader in her department. Interestingly, the offending staff found other positions and moved on and the ward attracted more dedicated professional staff.

Janine set new standards, applied herself daily and quickly inspired her team to raise their game.

Janine self-reported a deepening sense of integrity in her role and importantly, said that leadership felt natural and intuitive.

If this was an isolated case I'd never bother to document it. But over the last 20 years professionals worldwide like Janine consistently report that their ability to lead improved dramatically because they have simple tools that enable them to lead congruently, naturally and intuitively.

Please road-test the above questions for yourself and let me know what happens.

Andrew Priestley a multi-award winning business leadership coach. He is *Dent UK's* head coach and was listed in the *Top 100 UK Entrepreneur Mentors, 2017.*

Qualified in *Education* and *Industrial and Organisational Psychology* he has a wealth of business experience and has written three *#1 Amazon* bestselling books *The Money Chimp, Starting* and *Awareness.*

Web	*www.andrewpriestley.com*
Email	*info@andrewpriestley.com*
Twitter	*@ARPriestley*

Join Leadership Gigs

Would you like to be a part of *Leadership Gigs*? *Leadership Gigs* is a conversation for leaders worldwide. Here's how it works.

Think of it like a private members club – you can dip in and dip out as you wish – there is no pressure to show up.

Currently it is free to join. A good way to get involved is by starting with the *Facebook* group:

http://bit.ly/LeadershipGigsFB

Leadership Gigs is a support network so if you need high-end help/support then ask the group (you'll be nicely surprised). Our aim for this is to build a thriving community of leaders who are helping each other's journey into the next decade.

Our goal is to use our influence and skills to solve important problems. You may want to acquaint your self with the *United Nations Global Goals*.

http://www.globalgoals.org

In conclusion, thank you for purchasing *Fit-For-Purpose Leadership #1*. I would like to hear how you benefitted.

Watch out for *Fit-For-Purpose Leadership #2*, coming soon!

Lightning Source UK Ltd.
Milton Keynes UK
UKHW02f2356120118
316063UK00005B/204/P